D0570089

Part 1: Find Your Dreams

*D*reams are vitally important. They inspire us, help us grow, and give us hope. Our ability to dream stems from our ability to create, to imagine something that isn't and turn it into something that is. That is so powerful.

You will have thousands of dreams over the course of your lifetime—some small and simple, others huge and complex. But no matter the size, the principle remains the same. Every dream starts as an idea, a longing for something that isn't real yet.

Think of everything you've accomplished in your life that started out as a tiny dream. When you were little, you dreamed of riding your bike through your neighborhood, a taste of freedom with the wind in your hair. As you grew older, maybe you dreamed about making an athletic team or joining a prestigious club. Once you became an adult, your dreams became bigger—landing the job you wanted, starting a family, or buying a house.

For every dream that's come true, you've had to make a choice to pursue it. You've had to name that dream and decide that it is worth your hard work and effort to see it through. But you can't pursue a dream if you don't acknowledge that you have it.

If you know something is missing in your life and you want a change, you must start by diving into your dreams. It all starts with searching your heart, sifting through the myriad of dreams you've secreted away over time. Some will be dreams you've outgrown, and some won't be quite ready yet for you to pursue, but somewhere in your heart, there are God-given passions you've been longing for, and they're waiting for you to pull them out and pursue them.

1

Start Dreaming

The simple believes everything, but the
prudent gives thought to his steps.
PROVERBS 14:15 ESV

Every dream starts somewhere, but if you don't already have a dream, it can be difficult to know where to start. Dreaming, like anything else that truly matters, takes time.

It can be so easy to get caught up in the busyness of everyday life—work, the gym, groceries, making dinner, laundry—and, before you know it, each day is gone, and you still feel as lost as you did when you got up in the morning. But there is a dream inside of you just waiting for you to nourish it and help it grow. It's already there. You just have to find it.

Proverbs 14:15 tells us that if we are wise we will give thought to our steps. So, let's start there. To give thoughts to your steps fully, you have to give yourself space and time to do that thinking. Put dreaming time on your calendar.

There is a dream inside of you waiting for you to nourish it.

Commit to thirty minutes each morning to dream before you start your day, but if you don't know how you'll spare that much time, start with ten or fifteen minutes. Or set aside a weekend for a dreaming staycation to kick-start your dream journey. Whatever you do, find a comfortable, quiet spot with no distractions; stock it with pens, paper, or a notebook; and let yourself focus on dreaming.

Start each dreaming session with a prayer, asking God for wisdom and for Him to show you the dreams He has already hidden in your heart.

Here are some questions to get you started:

What do I love to do?

....

....

What are things I am very good at?

....

....

When I picture my future, what does it look like?

....

....

What are some things I've always wanted to do?

....

....

What type of lifestyle would I like to have?

....

....

When are times I've felt God nudging me to action?

....

....

When I pray for guidance, what do I feel God leading me toward?

....

2

You Were Created for Good Works

We are his workmanship, created in Christ Jesus for good works, which God prepared beforehand, that we should walk in them.

EPHESIANS 2:10 ESV

We were not made to go through life just treading water, barely surviving. Ephesians 2:10 tells us that God made each of us for good works. Those dreams bubbling up inside of you are some of the good works God is expecting from you!

Write out every dream you have for yourself, both over-the-top big and teeny, tiny small.

....

....

....

....

....

....

....

....

Which of those dreams would you describe as good works? Before you dismiss your desire to design your own fashion line, good works can come in many different forms. Not everyone dreams of becoming the next Mother Teresa, and that's okay. There are countless ways to do good in this world.

Let's approach this a little differently. Which of your dreams will allow you to help or to encourage others? To share the good news of Jesus? To love your neighbors? Which of your dreams can you approach with a heart full of love and passion to make a difference?

Good works come from the heart.

Good works come from the heart. You could dedicate your life to building orphanages, but if your heart isn't in it, then that isn't a good work for you (1 Corinthians 13:3). But if fashion lights you up inside, your dream to start a fashion line could be your calling. You could help tear down unfair beauty standards that contribute to eating disorders. You could commit to producing garments in clean factories where workers are treated ethically, providing needed jobs. You could donate profits to charities. There are a lot of options; the key is finding the right option for *your* dream.

Most dreams aren't inherently good or bad; it's the love in our hearts as we work for God that makes our dreams into the good works we are created for.

3

Embrace Your Gifts

In his grace, God has given us different
gifts for doing certain things well.
ROMANS 12:6 NLT

Each of us has our own unique strengths, things that we do well naturally. If you aren't sure which dream to go for, it may be time to genuinely assess your particular gifts. Those gifts are little signposts from God, leading you toward roles you are well suited for.

> God equips you for your dreams.

You will have a lot of dreams during your life. Only a few of those will line up perfectly with your talents and temperaments, as if they were made just for you. It only makes sense that if God has planted a dream in your heart, He will have equipped you with everything you need to make it real. These dreams will feel different when you really examine them. They will feel like a part of you, something undeniable that you can't ignore. If you find yourself torn between different dreams, ask yourself which one plays to your strengths, or which one is tugging at you the most right now.

Use this prayer as a way to thank God for the dreams He's given specifically to you and to ask Him for guidance on how to embrace them. Speak this prayer exactly as it is, or adapt it to your special needs and desires.

Heavenly Father,

Help me to discover the dreams that You have planted in my heart. Those are the dreams that I want to chase. Sometimes I feel so many different dreams and passions pulling at me that I struggle to figure out which ones come from You. I want to see more clearly which dreams are a natural fit for my personality because I know that You wouldn't have given me dreams that don't play to my strengths.

Thank You for all of the gifts You have given me. I appreciate the strengths (and the weaknesses!) that You made a part of my personality. I'm so glad that You made me this way. Please grant me the wisdom to clearly see the gifts You have blessed me with and help me to spot all of the ways I can use those gifts. I want to use them to do Your work.

In Jesus' name, amen.

4

You Don't Have to Be Qualified

We are confident of all this because of our great trust in God through Christ. It is not that we think we are qualified to do anything on our own. Our qualification comes from God.

2 CORINTHIANS 3:4–5 NLT

Are you quick to dismiss certain dreams out of fear, the ones that seem too big, too difficult, or just too much of a reach? Maybe you fear that you don't have what it takes? If you don't try, you can't fail, right? But unless your dream requires you to have an advanced degree that you don't have (kind of difficult to become a brain surgeon without going to medical school!), who's to say that you aren't qualified if God says you are?

Every world changer started out just like you.

Every single world changer out there started off just like you, a regular person with a big dream. To make those dreams into a reality, they had to be willing to get their hands dirty, figure things out, work hard, fail a few times and get back up, and have faith. They trusted that God would help them learn as they went, and He did.

Women who have never been to business school are CEOs

of the companies they built. Teenagers are running non-profits between studying for the SATs. Kids who have survived abusive childhoods grow up to become loving parents. They've all made mistakes and messed up in the process, but every misstep helped them learn what they needed to know. Just because you don't feel qualified now doesn't mean you can't get there in the process of chasing your dream.

What's holding you back from your big dream? Write out all of your reasons for why you think you aren't capable, and then ask God to send teachers and guidance your way.

....

....

....

....

....

5

No Dream Is Too Big

*May he give you the desire of your heart
and make all your plans succeed. May
we shout for joy over your victory and lift
up our banners in the name of our God.
May the LORD grant all your requests.*

PSALM 20:4–5

Do you feel like your dream is too wild? It's not. It's just that God-size dreams require God-size faith. God wants to give you the desires of your heart, desires that He whispered to you when you were created.

You aren't being too bold or presumptuous asking God to grant the desires of your heart. You are asking to become God's partner, letting Him write His story through you. You see only a few paragraphs of the epic story that God is writing, but God has a wonderful, fulfilling plan for you. While you might feel like your dream is too far-reaching, God already knows all of the ways He can use it in His story.

> God-size dreams require God-size faith.

When you work with God, impossible things suddenly become possible, and doors that were shut swing open wide. None of us can make that happen, but He can. Talk to God about those great, big dreams in your heart. Boldly approach Him, knowing He can make anything possible. Use this prayer as a place to start the conversation.

> *Father God,*
>
> *I want to share with You the deepest desires of my heart. I know that You already know what they are, but I believe that You want to hear from me. You want me to come to You with my dreams. I want to share how my dreams make me feel, how nervous I am about making them real, and how important my dreams are to me.*
>
> *As I go for this, I want You beside me. I want You to be my sounding board, my encourager, and my partner. I will work hard, but I know there will be plenty I can't do without You. There will be hurdles to overcome and times when I feel ready to quit. Those are the times when I will need You the most. Please stay with me and let me feel Your presence as I work. It comforts me to know I can count on You.*
>
> *In Jesus' name, amen.*

6

Narrow Down Your Dreams

A person's steps are directed by the LORD. How then can
anyone understand their own way? It is a trap to dedicate
something rashly and only later to consider one's vows.

PROVERBS 20:24–25

Some dreams are big; some are small. Some are there for a day, and some stick with you for years before you can make them come true. Throughout your life, you'll have many dreams. Some are specific to your age and experiences at the time, and other dreams are temporary or circumstantial or waiting for you to gather all you need to accomplish them. Because you'll have so many dreams, you can't possibly go after all of them! So how do you choose which ones to go for and which ones to let fade away?

> Your dreams are linked together.

Start with prayer. Ask God for His wisdom. Then, write down all of your current dreams. Once you've done that, circle the ones that would break your heart if they never happened. What do these dreams have in common? Do you see a pattern?

....

....

....

You will see something that links all of your dearest dreams together. But if you don't, take a break and come back with fresh eyes or ask a trusted friend to help you look over your list.

Once you see the connection, create a statement with those dreams in mind. If your dreams focus on writing and sharing stories, your statement might be, "My dreams allow me to tell stories, my own and other people's." If your dreams all center around creative endeavors, it could be, "My dreams help me to bring more beauty into the world." Write your statement below.

....

....

....

....

Are there dreams on your list that don't fit with the others? Those could be dreams to let go of. This will help you narrow down your dreams and focus on the direction where God is sending you right now.

1

Dreaming with Wisdom

*Do not forsake wisdom, and she will protect
you; love her; and she will watch over you. The
beginning of wisdom is this: Get wisdom. Though
it cost all you have, get understanding.*

PROVERBS 4:6–7

When you are jump-out-of-your-seat-excited about what you are planning to do, it's easy to race to get started instead of thinking things through. But no matter how excited you are, you can't leave wisdom at the door.

"Though it cost all you have, get understanding" is a clear command in today's key verse. Running full throttle for your dreams when you don't understand where they come from or what they mean, or you don't have a clear picture of where they will take you is a mistake.

Don't leave wisdom at the door.

Before you take a single step, have a prayerful conversation with God to make sure that this dream is from Him. The next step is to make a plan. Map out your dream. Write down the action steps you will need to follow. Then ask yourself the difficult questions:

What will it take from you (and others!) to make this dream come true?

....

....

Will it pull you away from other commitments and responsibilities?

....

....

Are you truly willing to sacrifice that much?

....

....

How will pursuing this dream impact other areas of your life?

....

....

Is this dream so all-consuming that it poses a danger of becoming an idol in your heart?

....

....

It is absolutely acceptable to want something deeply and to commit a lot of time and hard work to get it, but you can't let any dream become more important than your walk with God. However, if you take the time to confirm the dream with God, pursuing it will enrich your life and faith, rather than overtaking them or leading you astray. Then you can confidently step forward, trusting that you have God's wisdom to guide you.

8

Finding Purpose

O brothers and sisters loved by God,
we know He has chosen you.

1 THESSALONIANS 1:4 THE VOICE

So many of the dreams that drive each of us come down to one simple concept—purpose. Each of us is searching for our role in this crazy world, the ways that we can make an impact, the calling that God has chosen for us. The real question then is: How do you find your purpose?

If you already know your purpose, do a celebratory dance and then get busy fulfilling it. If you are still seeking or struggling to know how even to start finding your purpose, take heart. God tells us that He has chosen each of us. He has a role for you to play, and the key to finding your purpose and role is already inside you.

Your purpose drives your dreams.

Close your eyes for a few minutes and think about the world. Think about people in your community, in your country, in other countries. Think about all of the issues you see on the news or on social media. Have you seen or heard something that filled you with hope? Is there a cause or a group that stirs your heart and makes you want to take action? Think about what fills your heart with joy, what spurs your creativity, and what makes you feel most alive.

Write those things down here:

....

....

....

....

....

....

Once you have your list, look for commonalities. You might have a few outliers, but you should see a theme emerging. Your purpose very likely has something to do with these common issues and feelings. Pray about the themes you see and listen to see where God is calling you.

Now go back to your list of dreams you wrote previously. Which dreams align with the purpose you see emerging here? When those two areas align, those are the dreams that God can use to make a life-changing impact through you.

9

Go Bigger

"For assuredly, I say to you, whoever says to this
mountain, 'Be removed and be cast into the sea,'
and does not doubt in his heart, but believes
that those things he says will be done, he will
have whatever he says. Therefore I say to you,
whatever things you ask when you pray, believe
that you receive them, and you will have them."

MARK 11:23–24 NJKV

There is no dream that is impossible with God. All God asks of you is to have faith in Him.

It can be so easy to underestimate God, as if He has your human limitations because you can't realistically comprehend all that He can do. What a mistake it is to put limitations on God's power!

> No dream is impossible with God.

Of course, God is capable of expanding outside of any box you might try to put Him in, but oftentimes He waits patiently for you to realize that. He lets you make your dreams and life smaller and smaller until you finally, feeling lost and weary, turn to Him for help and guidance.

Instead of shrinking your passions, hopes, and ambitions, step forward with faith and dedicate yourself to going bigger. Use this prayer to tell God you're ready to challenge yourself, to dream bigger, and to trust that there is no limit to what God can do with your dreams.

Yahweh,

I want to live my biggest possible life. I think too small sometimes—a bad habit I want to break. I also make You too small in my mind. It's hard for me to truly understand everything You are. Thanks for reminding me when I make my world too narrow.

Please help me to go bigger—to notice bigger opportunities, take bigger risks, and serve You in bigger ways. Help me to spot ways to supersize my dreams. And please help me to have the courage to actually do it. Living small feels safe and familiar. Living big can feel too scary and risky. But I know big will be breathtaking and wonderful with You.

Please come alongside me, and expand my dreams into epic proportions. I'm ready.

In Your Son's name, amen.

10

Dreams Give Us Life

*Hope deferred makes the heart sick, but
a longing fulfilled is a tree of life.*

PROVERBS 13:12

Dreams aren't just wishes or hopes that never come true. Dreams motivate you, inspire you, and challenge you to grow. Without them, life would be ordinary and boring! Having something exciting to work toward helps breathe new life into your existing routines and responsibilities and also encourages you to step outside of your comfort zone to try new things and meet new people.

A dream should fill your stomach with butterflies.

If you are feeling down or stuck in a rut, it may be that you are missing the zing of having a dream to drive you. It could be that you have outgrown the dreams you've been working toward. Maybe you achieved a dream, and you're wondering, *Now what?* Or maybe you've been chasing the wrong dream and need to reassess.

Go back to that list of dreams you made previously.

As you reread them, ask yourself: Which dreams make me feel energized and excited? Which dreams don't create a spark inside of me?

....

....

....

....

....

A dream that doesn't fill your stomach with excited butterflies is likely one that you can let go of. But the dreams that make you want to get up early to get more work in, to take a risk, and to put yourself out there in new ways are dreams that are going to make your life bolder, brighter, and more inspired.

It's absolutely okay to prioritize the dreams that light you up, even if they don't seem as important or practical as others on your list. It's also okay to make time for these dreams during your "regular" life. Dreams bring new life and energy to everything, even your daily routines.

11

Make Plans

Careful planning puts you ahead in the long run;
hurry and scurry puts you further behind.
PROVERBS 21:5 THE MESSAGE

You wouldn't attempt to build a house without detailed plans, right? So why would you treat building your dreams any differently? It is important to do your research and make sure you really understand exactly what your dream will require of you, so that you don't get halfway down the road only to discover that this particular dream doesn't work well or fit anymore with your life.

Your plans will vary depending on what your dream is, of course. You might find you need to research, read books, and look for mentors in your desired field. If you are dreaming of starting your own business, you'll need to make a financial plan, lay out action steps for securing financing, put together lists of contacts and vendors, and research business licenses and laws for your state. If your dream is to become a successful artist, you'll need to plan to secure and build a website, decide what you'll create and how much, consider how you'll share your work and where, and research the best support system and audience for your creative pursuits.

Learn as much as you can.

Thinking about all of this might feel overwhelming, but it doesn't have to be. Oftentimes the first best step is to learn as much as you can!

Start by jotting down a list of everything you can think of that you may need to research. Then take one item on your list each day to work on further.

Within a few weeks, you should have the outlines of a plan in place. Now with your plan in place, pray about it, asking God for His wisdom and insight as you continue to move forward. Write down what dream you'd like to focus on, and jot down a few items you can research in the coming month. You don't have to be elaborate and detailed right now. Get a framework in place so you can take those first few steps toward your dream.

....

....

....

....

....

....

....

....

12

Identify Your Strengths and Weaknesses

*Examine yourselves, to see whether you
are in the faith. Test yourselves.*
2 CORINTHIANS 13:5 ESV

It's tough to be honest with yourself, but it's something you need to get comfortable with if you're going to chase big dreams. You've got to be crystal clear about your time, your resources, how difficult your challenges will be, and your strengths and weaknesses. God has blessed you with gifts, and dreams that come from Him always make excellent use of those gifts.

You are blessed with gifts.

Start by being honest about your strengths. Write down what you feel your greatest strengths are here.

....

....

....

....

....

....

Everyone has weaknesses too, so there's no shame in admitting yours here.

....

....

....

Think about the plans you wrote down about your dream. How will your strengths help you? How will your weaknesses hinder your progress?

....

....

....

If you see places in your plan that will require skills that you don't have, seek guidance. Reach out to a friend who's great at social media marketing to teach you about SEOs. Call up your mom's friend who's an accountant for a brief discussion about bookkeeping and tax laws. Visit your library for books that can help or register for an online class or seminar. Don't let your current lack of skills or knowledge be a deterrent from a dream you know you should pursue. There are lots of ways to grow your skills.

Also remember that there may be areas that just aren't for you. Take a moment to extend yourself some grace. Ask for help. Hire someone to take on the tasks that aren't where your strengths lie. Optimize your time doing what you are best at and build a community to help you with the rest!

13

Test Your Plans

Test everything; hold fast what is good.
1 THESSALONIANS 5:21 ESV

Once you have an action plan for pursuing one of your dreams, it's time to run it past someone you trust, someone who will give you good advice. Look for someone savvy and practical who also takes calculated risks and embraces change. Talk with someone you can trust to be honest with you without crushing your enthusiasm.

Use this prayer below as a way to prepare for the meeting, and ask for wisdom and vision.

> *Heavenly Father,*
>
> *I've been working so hard, and I want this so much. I know I'm biased. Please help me to walk into this meeting with an open heart and mind. Help me to hear feedback clearly, uncolored by my emotions. Please grant me the vision to know which feedback I should use and which I can let go of. Please show me clearly which parts of my plan are good and which need more work. I am willing to do the work. I am open to the wisdom.*
>
> *In Jesus' name, amen.*

Share your dreams and plans with your trusted friend, and be honest. Then listen with an open mind to their feedback. This is someone who cares about you, right? Someone who wants what's best for you, right? They aren't going to tear down your ideas for no reason, so listen closely.

Drill down to discover the parts of your plan that are solid and good. Keep those, but be willing to scrap anything that doesn't hold up to scrutiny. It might be the difference between a dream that dies and one that comes true.

God will show you the good parts of your plan and where it needs more work.

It's much easier to go back to the drawing board now, so take the time to plan, get feedback, pray, plan some more, get more feedback, pray on repeat, and so on until you have a plan that is worth holding on to.

14

Examine Your Dreams

It is pleasant to see dreams come true, but fools
refuse to turn from evil to attain them.

PROVERBS 13:19 NLT

Dreams that come from God won't require you to turn from Him to achieve them. If you find yourself in positions where you feel the need to lie, cheat, or steal to keep your dreams on track, it's unlikely this dream is really from God.

When you've poured your time, energy, and heart into a dream, it can be surprisingly easy to justify a few half-truths, then a few lies, and then cheating someone to cover up your wrongdoing. In the moment, that first half-truth can seem like no big deal. But even a trivial half-lie is a lie. Once you've set foot off the path with God, it's a steep and slippery slope down, and that fall isn't a matter of *if,* but *when.*

> **Dreams from God require His help to achieve them.**

Chasing big dreams means you might be placed in situations with all kinds of people, including the wrong sort. But God will always give you an escape route (1 Corinthians 10:13). If you stay mindful, you will be listening and looking for those little nudges from God that show you the way out. Say the prayer below as a way to ask God to help you examine your dreams.

Lord,

I want this dream to become real so badly. I'm sure that it probably clouds my judgment sometimes. Please help me to keep my eyes open and my wits about me. There are so many choices and options, and I can't always tell immediately which ones are right. But You always know, and I pray that You will help me see it all clearly too.

I know I will be tempted to take the easy way, even the wrong way. I'll get tired and a shortcut will seem so appealing. I need Your strength and wisdom to help me stay on the right path. I want to do this with You, the right way.

In Your Son's name, amen.

15

Ask for God's Input

*If any of you lacks wisdom, you should ask
God, who gives generously to all without
finding fault, and it will be given to you.*

JAMES 1:5

At the end of the day, you will have to make the decisions about your dream on your own. Friends can give advice and help, but only you can know if this dream is from God. Only you can experience His nudges that will alert you to an exciting opportunity or help you choose the right way when you come to a fork in the road.

> **Place your hopes in God, and He will lift your dreams higher.**

So it's also up to you to keep God in the loop. He wants to hear from you. He wants you to invite Him in, to welcome Him as your partner in achieving this dream.

God invites you into a wonderfully intimate relationship with Him. He can't wait to celebrate with you and help you, and He genuinely wants you to bring your troubles and sorrows to Him so that He can share His wisdom. He wants you to place your hopes in Him, because when you do, He can take your dreams to a higher level.

Take a moment to picture all of the hopes you have tied to your dreams, all of the things you want to happen as a result of them. Write them here.

....

....

....

....

....

....

....

....

Mark this page so that you can find it easily later. Once you have achieved one of your dreams, come back here. If you have been dreaming with God, it is a certainty that you will have achieved so much more than what you wrote down. Because no matter how well prepared you are, you can never see the whole, gigantic picture that God sees. You can't even comprehend all the things that you don't know, which is why you need to include God in all of your planning. Your dreams need God's wisdom and vision.

Dream with God, and He will bless you with His wisdom.

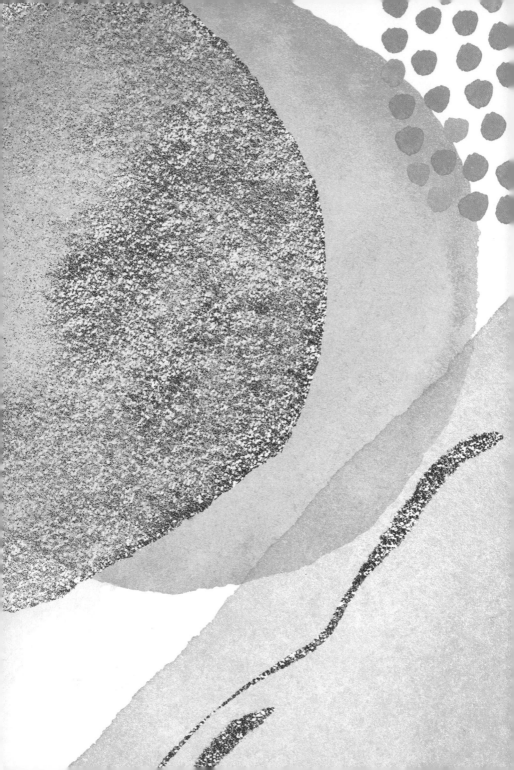

Part 2: God's Dreams for You

God created each and every one of us for a purpose. He gifts us dreams to help us uncover and pursue our purpose and to do our part in seeing it realized. God's dreams for us are beautiful. They will challenge us, help us grow, and fill us with faith.

God plants His dreams for you in your heart. The word used most often in the New Testament for heart is *kardia,* a Greek word that translates "the real you." Scripture uses the word heart to mean your internal motivations, your love, and your passions. God's dreams for you flow from all of that, from the way He made you. God's dreams for you won't be anything like His dreams for anyone else because He creates dreams that are specific to you, dreams that take advantage of your unique combination of strengths, experiences, and passions.

Of course, you will have dreams that don't come from God too. You've been dreaming your whole life, and you'll discard more dreams than you pursue. You'll also have dreams that aren't related to your purpose. None of that is bad, but in that constant swirl of dreams, it can be difficult to figure out which ones are from God and which ones you need to let go of.

Determining God's dreams for you requires wisdom and serious, intentional soul-searching. Here are a few key questions you can ask to get started: Does this dream contradict God's Word? Will this dream help others? Does this dream require faith?

God's dreams for you won't require you to turn away from His teachings, and they won't be selfish. Most importantly, if you can accomplish a dream by yourself, no faith is required. God's dreams for you are so big that you can't pursue them alone and will need to draw closer to God to see them through.

16

Where Did Your Dream Come From?

From heaven the LORD looks down and sees all
mankind; from his dwelling place he watches
all who live on earth—he who forms the hearts
of all, who considers everything they do.

PSALM 33:13–15

Some dreams arise out of a situation we've walked through, some come from others' expectations of us, and still others seem to leap into our minds, fully formed. No matter how it happened, where your dreams come from matters.

Take a few minutes to really think about the moment when that passion was born.

When did you first feel that tiny spark? How did you feel when you realized that this was *the* dream? Write it all out below, every detail you can remember.

....

....

....

....

Your dreams and passions were created when you were. Psalm 33:13–15 says that God formed each of our hearts and that He considers everything that we do. That passion was woven into every part of you.

God thought about everything you would do and how you would do it. He knows how you are wired because He wired you! He gave you a heart that He knew would break for orphans crying out for their mothers and a soul that He knew would delight in the boundless creativity of music. He designed your dreams to be a part of all that.

Your dreams and passions were created when you were.

Ask God why He gifted you with this particular passion. Then be still and pay attention for His answers. Those answers will help you define your purpose, fuel you when you get tired, and clothe you in the confidence you need for this journey.

If you already know why God gave you your dream, write it here. If you aren't sure, keep asking and waiting patiently for God's answer. You'll *know* when He answers.

....

....

....

....

....

17

God Has Plans for You

"For I know the plans I have for you," declares
the LORD, "plans to prosper you and not to harm
you, plans to give you hope and a future."
JEREMIAH 29:11

Having a plan is essential to getting your dream off the ground, but you have to be careful to hold those plans loosely, knowing that they must be flexible and able to change as circumstances change. And circumstances *will* change. That's all but guaranteed.

There's an old saying, "Make a plan and God laughs." There's a good reason for that, and it's definitely not that God, in His infinite wisdom, is sitting around cracking up at your attempts to make things happen. The real heart of that saying is that God's plans are always better than your plans. He knows so much more than you know, and He sees so much more than you see. His plans account for every variable, every possibility, every potential roadblock.

God's plans are the best plans.

You can choose to feel frustrated about the fact that your plans don't work out the way you'd hoped, or you can lean into the promise that God's plans will give you a hope and a future. If having a plan you've devised can help you feel more organized, then how much more comforting is it to know that God has a plan He's laid out just for you to prosper?

Think back to times when you've made plans that didn't turn out how you hoped. How did God turn those moments around? How did He make His plans known instead? Write it out here and come back to it when you need a reminder that God always has your greatest good in mind.

....

....

....

....

....

....

....

....

....

....

....

18

Seek God's Dreams for You

Show me your ways, LORD, teach me your paths.
Guide me in your truth and teach me, for you are
God my Savior, and my hope is in you all day long.

PSALM 25:4-6

So what do you do if your dreams have crashed? Or if you feel like you've never really had a big dream? What if you've accomplished all of your dreams and you don't know what to do next?

> God answers when the time is perfect.

Maybe you have hundreds of dreams bouncing around in your head. Or maybe you don't. Maybe having dreams feels as rare as catching a glimpse of a falling star, brightness lighting up the night sky for just one shining moment.

If you find yourself dream-free, for whatever reason, it might mean that God is waiting for you. Set aside time each day to pray, to ask God to share His dreams for you. Then, and this is the most difficult part, wait patiently for the answer.

- Spend time in silence after you pray, keeping your thoughts still. Quiet your heart and mind. God will answer when the time is perfect.

- Try free writing. Start writing about your desires for a dream from God. Don't stop to revise, fix spelling errors, or erase anything. Just write whatever crosses your mind for twenty minutes. Go back and read what you wrote later. See if anything stands out or makes you feel a spark of an idea.
- Be mindful as you walk through your day. What is catching your attention? Is there anything that you can't stop thinking about? Something you start to see everywhere? Write it all down.

....

....

....

....

....

....

....

....

....

....

As you wait for God and see themes or ideas emerging, pray about those. God's ways are not always easy to see or understand, but God will guide you to His dream for you in His perfect timing. Continue to seek Him every day, and the path He has for you will be revealed, one step at a time.

19

God's Dreams Are Everlasting

The LORD foils the plans of the nations; he
thwarts the purposes of the peoples. But the plans
of the LORD stand firm forever, the purposes
of his heart through all generations.

PSALM 33:10–11

When you dream, you're probably thinking about yourself, your life, your work, or your legacy. Dreams are highly personal, after all. But when God dreams, He thinks about the generations who will come after you. He thinks of all of the other dreams that will be affected by your dream. He thinks of the lives that will be made better because of your dream. God is always playing the long game.

> God plays the long game, considering generations to come.

There is only so far into the future you can plan. It's okay that you are mostly playing the short game as long as you keep your eyes on God, because the dreams God places in your heart are everlasting. Use the prayer below as a way to say thank you to God for using the dreams in your heart to make a lasting and positive result on people you may never know.

Holy Father,

I know that there is so much more to Your plans and to the dreams that You have given me. It's more than I can see and understand. I'm okay with playing the short game. Thank You for playing the long game.

I know that Your plans echo down through time, revealing Your goodness long after I'm gone. I don't have to know all the things You plan to do with my dreams; I just have to trust and have faith that You are going to take them so much further than I ever could. Help me to keep my faith strong. Help me to remember that I can trust You to carry this dream long after I'm gone.

I hope that one day I can stand beside You and You can show me all of the beautiful things You have done with this dream.

In Your Son's name, amen.

20

God's Purpose + Your Passion

*For in him all things were created: things in
heaven and on earth, visible and invisible, whether
thrones or powers or rulers or authorities; all things
have been created through him and for him.*

COLOSSIANS 1:16

All things have been created through God and for Him, including you, your dreams, and your purpose. His fingerprints are on all of it. The purpose that God has planted in you is really His purpose, a little bit of His heart that He chose to share with you. His love and sense of justice made new again in you.

God has filled you with His purpose.

When you can identify that purpose and combine it with your dreams and your passions, the impact those dreams will have on the world will be amplified in a big way. There are a lot of ways for God's purpose and your passions to make a difference. You can:

- donate a portion of your profits or salary to a charity that speaks to your purpose.
- ask your company to consider matching any charitable donation you make.

- ask your coworkers to join you on a volunteer day.
- consider donating unsold inventory at the end of each season if you own your own company.
- hire people who might not be offered chances at other companies.
- share about the causes that matter to you on your social media platform.

We weren't put here to sit on the sidelines and play it safe. God shared His purpose with you because He wants you to love Him, love one another, and engage in meaningful work that helps you do both. If your dreams have been leaving you feeling lackluster, it might be because passion alone can't sustain you. You need the purpose God has given you to really light you up inside. Think of ways you can combine God's purpose and your passions and start this week to implement them. Notice how your life starts to change.

21

Give Back

A generous person will prosper; whoever
refreshes others will be refreshed.

PROVERBS 11:25

All of us can get tunnel vision when it comes to pursuing our dreams. Our plans, our needs, our next moves—it's more than enough to keep our planners full, right? But God doesn't give you selfish dreams, so if your dream is all about you, you, you, then you are missing something of crucial importance.

Scripture tells us over and over how important it is for you to love and care for one another. This isn't just for others' sakes, but for yours as well. You were made to live in community, to walk beside one another. To hold hands and share burdens, to lift each other up and celebrate together, and to help pick up the pieces and grieve when life gets tough.

You can't achieve your dreams on your own.

None of us ever achieves anything in this life all on our own. The things you are able to achieve today are only possible because of all the things accomplished by those who came before you. You get an assist from time to time from family, friends, or even strangers. Even if you don't think you need any help with your dream, the day will come when you will. Having a community of friends and colleagues to reach out to will be a glorious blessing when you need support, encouragement, and love from those around you. There might even be someone you know who needs assistance, and you might be able to help her with her dream *today*! Your skills, connections, or input could be just what a friend needs to get her plans off the ground.

Thinking about all the ways you've been helped may inspire ways you can lend a hand to someone else. How have others helped you achieve things in your life?

....

....

....

....

....

....

....

....

22

Let God Lead You

In their hearts humans plan their course,
but the LORD establishes their steps.

PROVERBS 16:9

While pursuing your dream, there will be times when you find yourself unsure of what to do next. And it will be frustrating. You'll find yourself up late planning or wracking your brain for how to get to the next step. But you may not be able to find the answers or the path by yourself.

Sometimes you have to let go of your plans and let God implement His. Waiting for God to establish your steps can be tough because waiting isn't easy or comfortable. But God always does things in His perfect time, and, if you let Him, He can show you the beauty in the waiting.

Let God lead you.

Many people think of waiting as time wasted, but that's not a sentiment that God shares. When God asked Abraham and Sarah to wait for a child, He knew they needed that time to accomplish a few things before they would be ready for that particular blessing. And by waiting until they were older, there was no mistaking where that baby blessing came from. Abraham and Sarah couldn't say her pregnancy was due to the natural order of things—not when she was nearly ninety and he was one hundred years old! God's timing showed them exactly how powerful He is, deepening their trust in Him.

What do you think God is teaching you in your season of waiting?

....

....

....

....

....

....

....

....

....

Having a plan is a wonderful thing and can save you from a lot of hardship, but no amount of planning can prepare you for everything. When you stall out, thank God for the pause and open your eyes to see what He might be showing you.

23

Rejoice in What God Has Already Done

Come and see what God has done, his
awesome deeds for mankind.

PSALM 66:5

God has been working in you every moment of your existence, but it is often easier to see His hand on your life when you step back for a wider view. All the detours, dead-ends, nudges, and diversions make so much more sense when looked at as a whole. Those setbacks, "lucky" breaks, epiphanies, and frustrations were God nudging you—okay, sometimes *shoving* you—onto the right track.

You are a miracle.

When you see all of that, it becomes impossible to say your path has been nothing but random chance or luck. Only the loving hand of the Divine could have orchestrated the unique blend of challenges, successes, failures, and learning opportunities that have made you who you are today, ready to accomplish this particular dream at this particular time. You are a miracle. Use the prayer below as a starting point for thanking God for all He has done and for praising Him for His blessings and detours in your life.

Heavenly Father,

You have blessed me abundantly. I am so grateful for all of the opportunities You have given me, the family and friends who love me, and the way You take care of me, even in the toughest of times. I know that I don't even fully know all of the times and ways that You have looked out for my well-being. I am so grateful for Your love and guidance.

Please continue to nurture gratitude in my heart. I get caught up in the business of everyday life, and I sometimes forget just how much I have to be thankful for. Working to accomplish new and bigger dreams isn't bad, but I never want to forget just how much I already have and who gave it all to me—You. Thank You!

In Jesus' name, amen.

24

Check in with God Every Day

In the morning, O Eternal One, listen for my
voice; in the day's first light, I will offer my prayer
to You and watch expectantly for Your answer.
PSALM 5:3 THE VOICE

God wants to hear from you. He can see exactly what's happening in your life, but He created you to live your life *with* Him. He wants to hold you through your problems, your worries, and your heartbreaks and celebrate with you in your successes, realizations, and joyful moments. But it's not during only the highs and lows when God wants to hear from you; He wants to hear your observations about the world and people around you, laugh at your witty jokes, and hang out with you as you navigate through your most ordinary days. God loves you even at your most mundane.

God wants to hear from you.

Isn't that great news? A lot of life is made up of the mundane—laundry, cooking, spreadsheets, commuting, running errands—and God is with you through it all. So why would you only talk to Him for a few minutes each day? Or every other day? Or only during extreme moments, highs or lows?

God wants to hear from you more than that. Prayers don't have to be formal and stiff. You can talk to God all day long, out loud, or in your head. He will always hear you. He's with you already, so invite Him into your mundane and messy. Sing along with Him in the car. Laugh with Him at your latest cooking disaster. Plan your dreams with Him on your break. And commiserate with Him over your little one's new phrase over dinner. He wants to hear it all.

Write a prayer of your own, something personal to share with God. Tell Him about your day, your thoughts, and that great joke your boss told this morning. Share the richness of your life with Him.

....

....

....

....

....

....

....

....

....

....

....

....

25

Give It to God

Commit to the LORD whatever you do,
and he will establish your plans.
PROVERBS 16:3

Are you ready to be brave and bold? To walk to the edge of the figurative cliff and jump, trusting that God won't let you fall?

Then it's time to give your dream to God, to let go and have complete faith that He will lead you exactly where you need to be. It's time to fully commit your life—all of your hopes and dreams—to God.

Commit your dreams to God.

Part of following Jesus, even when it's uncomfortable, is committing your life, your plans, and your dreams to God and His use. If you are only pursuing your dreams on your terms, to fit into the life you envision for yourself, you haven't fully committed to God. It's a daunting step, to be sure, because it's a step of ultimate faith and surrender. You know that when you give it all to God, it's possible that He could take apart your dreams or remake them into something totally different. But when you give it all to God, you are trusting that He will help you fly instead of letting you fall. Say the prayer below and give your dreams to God and see how magnificent He will make them.

Father God,

I am giving my dreams to You. I've been growing dreams in my heart and nurturing them with everything I have. Now I want to turn my dreams over to You. Take my dreams and make them bigger, better, and more. Use me and my dreams for Your purposes.

I will go where You send me and do whatever You ask, even if it makes me uncomfortable or embarrassed or challenges me in ways that I can't imagine yet. I want to become more like You, to follow Jesus more faithfully. I can only do that by giving all of this to You. My dreams are Yours and so am I.

In Jesus' name, amen.

26

Be Still

*He says, "Be still, and know that I am God; I will be
exalted among the nations, I will be exalted in the earth."*

PSALM 46:10

Today's verse from Psalms is one of the most comforting verses.
When all of your anxieties and worries run rampant, this is the
verse to turn to in your Bible. God doesn't ask
you to stay up all night overthinking everything
or to stress buy stuff you don't need. He says,
"Be still."

> **Embrace
> the quiet.
> Trust God is
> in control.**

There's a good reason you can buy eighty
different books on meditation at your local book-
store. It can be a challenge to calm your body
and mind to a reflective quiet. But the answer to
your stress is to embrace the quiet, to be still and know that God
has everything in control.

What are some ways you best achieve stillness?

....

....

....

....

....

Once you have found stillness, God commands you, "Know that I am God." God wants you to contemplate just what it means that He is God. He wants you to open your mind to try to understand how much power He wields, which is *all* the power. He wants you to find assurance by reminding yourself how much He can control, which is everything. He wants you to be comforted by the knowledge that God will outlast every nation, leader, and institution on earth—every single one. And He wants you to have complete faith that He has got this.

Running after dreams will challenge you. You will be plagued by worries, self-doubt, and fear as you put yourself out there. But God is bigger than your worries and more powerful than your fears. Be still and know that He is God and He's got you.

27

In Time

Yet God has made everything beautiful for its own time. He has planted eternity in the human heart, but even so, people cannot see the whole scope of God's work from beginning to end.

ECCLESIASTES 3:11 NLT

God's timing is perfect. He created each of us for the time we're living in right now. He created our dreams for specific times too. The dreams that helped you through tough times weren't accidents. And neither are dreams that are still growing in your heart. Those dreams will become clearer as their time grows near. God's dreams and His timing go hand in hand.

Perhaps you're guilty of trying to force God to work on your timetable instead of His. When you want something desperately, it's hard not to keep pushing until you get it. But forcing a dream to bloom before its time makes about as much sense as trying to get a baby to hurry up and get a job. As cute as that baby would be in a little suit sitting at a desk, they're not ready for a job, and nothing but time will change that.

God's dreams and timing are perfect.

For example, if you've been hitting dead-ends at every turn, consider serious reflection to see if you are rushing this dream before its time. What are some reasons you feel that the time for this dream is now? What are some reasons this dream may not be ready?

....
....
....
....
....
....
....
....

Keep praying and asking God to reveal His perfect timing to you for this dream. He has already planted it in your heart, but it will take honesty, wisdom, and patience to uncover all the steps needed for the success of this dream.

28

God's Plans Are Not the World's Plans

Don't copy the behavior and customs of this world, but let God transform you into a new person by changing the way you think. Then you will learn to know God's will for you, which is good and pleasing and perfect.

ROMANS 12:2 NLT

Our world doesn't always agree with God about anything. The world's idea of success includes wealth, power, and fame. God's idea of success is helping others and loving and obeying Him. Society's idea of beauty focuses on youth and perfection. God's idea of beauty is reflected in everything He has ever created, including you—no changes needed. Our culture's idea of love is conditional on the right behaviors and attractiveness. God's love is unconditional and never-ending.

> God's plans are not the world's plans.

Yet you've probably, at some time or another, built plans or made decisions based on the world's expectations. While you do have to live in the world, that doesn't mean your plans and dreams have to fit into society's idea of anything. When you partner with God on your dreams, He will change your ways of thinking about and seeing the world. Remember, God's plans are not the world's plans.

How are your dreams setting you apart from the world's expectations and ideas?

....

....

....

....

....

....

Other people may not understand where your dreams are going. If they aren't dreaming with God, they likely won't get it. But God doesn't change Himself to fit into the world, and He doesn't want you to either. Keep your eyes on God and keep going because God is using you and your dreams to make this world a little bit more like Him, and that is good and pleasing and perfect.

29

God Makes Things Happen

"Remember the former things, those of long ago; I am God, and there is no other; I am God, and there is none like me. I make known the end from the beginning, from ancient times, what is still to come. I say, 'My purpose will stand, and I will do all that I please.' From the east I summon a bird of prey; from a far-off land, a man to fulfill my purpose. What I have said, that I will bring about; what I have planned, that I will do."

ISAIAH 46:9-11

God not only sees what you can't see and knows what you can't know, but He also has the power to breathe life into things you once thought were dead and create miracles. So, when God says, "What I have said, that I will bring about; what I have planned, that I will do," you can trust that God's plans for you will unfold exactly as He wishes. He will bring together the people and circumstances to ensure that His plans succeed.

You can build your faith on God's promises.

You know that broken dream that you've written off as never going to happen? God can patch it together and make it new again. How about the roadblock you can't get past? God will push it aside, revealing a clear path ahead. Have you ever dreamed about that pie-in-the-sky contact who could open doors for you? God will be there to ensure your paths cross and the connection is made. There is nothing that God can't make happen.

God's promises are ones that you can build your faith on. They provide a firm foundation because His Word is absolute truth. Here are some other promises that You can build Your faith on:

- God loves you unconditionally (Romans 8:38–39).
- You are never alone (Psalm 27:10).
- God created you with a purpose (Psalm 139).
- God has good plans for you (Jeremiah 29:11).

You won't know or always understand God's plans, but you can trust in His promise that He will do all that He pleases and that His purpose will stand.

30

Trust God

*Trust in the LORD with all your heart, and lean
not on your own understanding; in all your ways
acknowledge Him, and He shall direct your paths.*

PROVERBS 3:5–6 NKJV

Unless your dream is extremely straightforward and easy to achieve, there will come a time when your journey takes you through what feels like the wilderness, and you'll have to walk forward blindly. Your dark night may be financial instability, disapproval from family or friends, not being admitted to a program you need to attend, or any number of other hurdles that seem insurmountable.

God has excellent vision.

Have you already found yourself walking blindly through the wilderness? Or is there an obstacle you know will be a dream killer and you're hoping you don't encounter it?

....

....

....

....

....

God has excellent night vision. When you are walking blindly, He sees as though the sun is shining in a clear sky. This is why God tells you to trust Him over and over again, to have complete faith. He will steer you around every pitfall and show you His detours to avoid those dream killers. But you have to trust Him to lead the way.

It's tempting to assume that you know best, that no one could care about your dreams as much as you do. Maybe you've even insisted on taking every step based on your feelings and on your limited knowledge. But God cares every bit as much about your dreams as you do. He isn't hampered by volatile emotions or a lack of knowledge when it comes to choosing the right path. He sees the whole picture—past, present, and future.

When you find yourself lost in the wilderness and walking blindly, lean on your faith. Let God lead you out of the darkness and into His bright, sunny morning.

Part 3: Follow Your Dreams

A dream that you keep only in your heart will always be just that, a dream. But the big dreams that come from God were always meant to be made real. For those dreams to come to life, you have to take a leap of faith and start doing the work to make them happen. It can be nerve-wracking, terrifying, and daunting to take that first step, but it will also be exhilarating. It always is when you are doing what you were made to do.

It can be tempting to put off this work until everything is perfect and you feel 100 percent ready to take the first step, but it will never feel perfect and you will never be completely ready. At some point, you have to go for it, even if it's a little messy and even if it makes you feel a little out of control. Because even if you aren't 100 percent ready, God is. And even if everything isn't absolutely perfect, God is. God will be right there beside you.

All you have to do is trust Him and get to work. You can do it.

31

Have Faith in Your Dreams

"If you have faith as small as a mustard seed, you can say to this mountain, 'Move from here to there,' and it will move."
MATTHEW 17:20

If you don't have faith in your dreams, how can you expect anyone else to? If you are constantly second-guessing your every decision, doubting your abilities, and suffering with anxiety, it will be next to impossible to have the kind of trust in yourself and in God that it takes to make big things happen.

Of course you'll have moments of uncertainty and anxiety because the world is far from perfect, but your faith in God and His dreams for you is what will keep you moving forward despite fear and doubt. When you're feeling uncertain and insecure, it's best to be proactive.

Have faith in your dreams.

Think of one dream you have. What are your fears, doubts, and concerns about your dream? Then, one by one find a verse in your Bible that is stronger than your fear. Anytime you feel those doubts creeping in, turn to the verse you've selected for an instant boost of faith from the Word of God.

32

Your Dreams Won't Work Unless You Do

Whatever you do, work at it with all your heart, as
working for the Lord, not for human masters.
COLOSSIANS 3:23

It will require a lot of hard work to take your dream from hypothetical into actuality. Even if you feel eager to get started, the work may still seem tricky to fit into your already jam-packed schedule. The truth is that if you want to give your dream all you've got, you will have to find things to remove from your calendar.

There are some responsibilities you won't be able to get out of—you still have to take care of your kids and walk your dog!—but there will be other time slots that can be repurposed, even if it's uncomfortable to do it. Skipping out on binge-watching your favorite TV show, brunch with your friends, or long, lazy weekends with your sweetheart will be worth it in the long run.

Think about ways you can prioritize working toward your dream here. It may mean saying no to activities you enjoy or sacrificing sleep to give you extra time for your dream work. Take a sincere look at your life and how you are choosing to spend your time. There is more wiggle room than you think to add in time for your dream, if you are willing to prioritize this dream that God has trusted you with.

33

Love What You Do

Delight attends her work and guides her fingers.
PROVERBS 31:13 THE VOICE

You've heard the old adage that if you love what you do, it will never feel like work. When you have a goal that you are passionate about, making it happen feels more like a privilege than a job. But, make no mistake, there will always be work to be done.

Find the balance between what you love and what challenges you.

Once you have your dream up and running, though, you will have the opportunity to choose which work you spend most of your time doing. Even passion projects include tasks that aren't as enjoyable as other aspects. If you want your dreams to continue and grow, it only makes sense to balance the tasks you love with the ones you're less fond of.

What do you love working on for your dream? What do you dread?

....

....

....

....

If you can afford to hire help with the tasks that feel like a drag on your energy and time, it could be an expense worth incurring. A carefully selected hire can free you up to focus on creating the vision for your dream's long-term success. Even if you're a one-woman shop, there are options. You can book a virtual assistant or outsource bookkeeping to a great accountant. If you have a creative community, consider trading your creative know-how for help from someone else's expertise (if time allows).

If delegating isn't in the cards for you just yet, setting your schedule with intention will help. Start your day with the tasks you dread. Get them out of the way! Or designate one day each week to knock out your least favorite to-dos. That will free up the rest of your week for the to-dos you can't wait to do. You know yourself best, so think through what will motivate you to tackle the more challenging tasks consistently and quickly, freeing you up to do what you love more often.

34

Run

I instruct you in the way of wisdom and lead you along
straight paths. When you walk, your steps will not be
hampered; when you run, you will not stumble.

PROVERBS 4:11–12

Being prudent and thoughtful are both important when making plans to go after a dream, but you'll likely reach a point where you have to trust your planning, trust God, and just go for it. Use this prayer to help bolster your courage to trust you've planned well and that it's now time to act.

Block out the noise from the world.

Heavenly Father,

I am so ready to run after this dream. We've talked about this so much and planned for it for so long together. I can see the path You've laid out for me, straight and true. As I take these first steps, picking up speed, please help me to trust the path and trust You.

I know I can't sprint the way I'm longing to if I keep looking out for potholes, bumps, and curves that aren't there. My heart says to trust that You have cleared the way, but my fears tell me always to be looking for the bad stuff, never to trust anything too much. I don't want my fears to win.

Please help to quiet my fears and calm my need to anticipate the worst. Block out the noise from the world that tells me, "You can't," so that I can more easily hear You telling me, "You can and you will." Open my eyes with trust that I may continue to see the path before me clearly. Fill me with joy as my feet pound against the path, the wind rushes across my face, and the sun shines down on my run. Set a steady pace for me please so that I can run and not grow weary alongside You.

In Jesus' name, amen.

35

When Your Goals Are His Goals

*"Seek first his kingdom and his righteousness, and
all these things will be given to you as well."*
MATTHEW 6:33

When you choose to dream with God, inviting Him into every part of your life, you will find your heart changing to become more like His. And, as a Christ follower, isn't that your ultimate goal? Ask God to dream with you and through you today. Use this prayer to talk to God about making your goals align with His goals, and ask Him to help you filter out the noise of the world so you can better see His path for you.

Invite God to dream with you.

Father God,

I love dreaming with You. I know that I could never have come up with my dreams on my own. Your vision for my life is perfectly designed, and I am so grateful that You created me as part of Your plan. I want to want what You want, and I want to do the things You have called me to do. Please help my heart to become more like Yours.

I know that I sometimes get it wrong. I am both Your child and a child of the world I was born into. What my culture tells me that matters, what it tells me I should want, and what it tells me to pursue are very, very loud and very different sometimes than what You tell me. I don't want to let down the people I love or feel ashamed for choosing a different way, but I hate the thought of letting You down even more. I only want to be Your child.

Please, Lord, work in my heart to filter out all of the noise of the world so that I can really hear Your truth. With my words and actions, dreams and goals, I want my identity as Your child to win out over my identity as a child of the world. Keep calling me to Your work, and keep drawing me closer to You.

In Your Son's name, amen.

36

Work with Confidence in Your Dreams

She has a plan. She considers some land and buys it; then with
her earnings, she plants a vineyard. She wraps herself in strength,
carries herself with confidence, and works hard, strengthening
her arms for the task at hand. She tastes success and knows it
is good, and under lamplight she works deep into the night.
PROVERBS 31:16–18 THE VOICE

While your dreams may not be what the Proverbs 31 woman's dreams were, you can still learn a lot from the way she pursued them. She went after what she wanted, trusting God to help her succeed.

Proverbs tells us that she is delighted by her work, provides for her family, plans wisely, and then executes those plans confidently. She takes thoughtful risks, such as buying land and investing to improve it. She designs and sells clothing. She enjoys success and works hard to achieve it. But she also helps those in need and speaks with wisdom and kindness. She trusts God and, as such, she has no fear of the future. She certainly sounds like a dreamer!

Work for your dreams with confidence.

What is most striking about the Proverbs 31 woman is that she works with confidence and has no fear of the future. She could be resentful of all the work she has to do or be too insecure and plagued by doubt to buy land or sell the clothes she has made, but instead she has serious faith in herself and in God. Faith enough to tackle all of that work with delight, unburdened by fear. How do you tackle your daily to-do list? With faith and confidence or with insecurity, doubt, and resentment?

Write down everything you do each day. I bet you'll find that you are achieving way more than you think. Which of these tasks are you doing with confidence and delight? Which with resentment and doubt?

....

....

....

....

....

....

....

....

....

....

....

31

Take Your Dreams Seriously

It pays to take life seriously; things work
out when you trust in GOD.
PROVERBS 16:20 THE MESSAGE

If you truly want to make your dreams a reality, you have to take them seriously. Choosing to chase a dream is a commitment you are making to yourself and to God, and your dream should carry just as much weight with you as any other commitment.

Would you be willing to skip out on a promise you made to your child? Or a task you took on for your boss? Of course not! No one likes to disappoint people. Then why are you so willing to let down yourself by putting your dreams at the bottom of your priority list?

Take your dreams seriously.

You're probably busy with your job, friends, and family. There are dozens of little tasks required to keep your life afloat. Sometimes the thought of cramming one more thing into your already packed schedule feels like too much. But the truth is that if you don't take your dreams seriously and prioritize those dreams in your schedule, there is a real chance that those dreams will become regrets.

Do you want to regret not ever writing that novel? Not ever auditioning for a Broadway show? Not ever going back to school for that degree you need for your dream job? Not starting that business?

What would you regret the most if your dream never became real?

....

....

....

....

....

....

....

It might be time to make a change. Block off time on your calendar every day when you are at your most productive to work on your dream. Get up early if you have to or stay up late. Take that lunch break you usually skip. Do what you have to do to find the time. Take your dreams seriously and feel confident that you will live without the regret of never pursuing them the way God wants you to. Make the change today.

38

Stick to Your Goals

I will press on—moving steadfastly forward along
Your path. I will not look back. I will not stumble.
PSALM 17:5 THE VOICE

When your dream feels overwhelming—and they will sometimes—it can really help to break them down into smaller
action steps, goals you can complete to keep your dreams moving forward. These goals can be as small or
as big as you like. You're the only one who
knows what will feel achievable to you.

**Create small
actions steps
for your
dreams.**

Choose a dream that rises to the surface
most often in your mind. Think about all
of your current goals for your dream here
and give each a due date. You'll have some
goals that you can't start quite yet or that
you can't tackle until you complete some of
your other goals, and that's okay. Set a due date to revisit that goal,
and see if you can set a real time line.

As you think about these goals, invite God into the process,
and listen to what He might be sharing with you. You don't want
to miss the chance to add a goal from God to your list!

39

Banishing Anxiety

"Why worry about your clothing? Look at the lilies of the field and how they grow. They don't work or make their clothing. . . . And if God cares so wonderfully for wildflowers that are here today and thrown into the fire tomorrow, he will certainly care for you."

MATTHEW 6:28, 30 NLT

Worrying is part of the human condition. We all do it, even though it doesn't do us any good. God knows this about us, and His Word is filled with verses to banish your fears and comfort you. The next time you feel anxiety creeping in and coloring your dreams with doubt, read these to find peace.

- 2 Timothy 1:7
- Isaiah 40:31
- Isaiah 41:10
- John 14:1
- Psalm 56:3
- Joshua 1:9
- Luke 12:22
- Psalm 34:4
- Matthew 6:27
- Hebrews 13:6
- Psalm 94:19
- Proverbs 3:5–6
- Jeremiah 17:7–8
- Philippians 4:6–7
- Luke 12:24–34
- John 14:27
- Psalm 55:22
- 2 Thessalonians 3:16
- Proverbs 12:25
- 1 Peter 5:7
- Psalm 23:4
- Isaiah 35:4

40

You Can Do Anything, but Not Everything

So teach us to number our days that
we may get a heart of wisdom.

PSALM 90:12 ESV

Anything is possible with God, truly anything. There is nothing that God can't make happen. And God can make anything happen for every single one of the 7.8 billion people around the world at the exact same time.

You are more limited in the quantity of what you can accomplish. Forget focusing on 7.8 billion things at once; you can really only do one thing at a time well. You also have needs you can't ignore, such as eating and sleeping. Your time and energy are limited.

With God you can achieve your dreams.

With God on your side, you can achieve anything He has called you to, but that doesn't mean you can do *everything*. Many people believe that they can do it all if they just try hard enough. The hard truth is that you have a choice each morning as to how you are going to spend your day. You can cram in as much stuff as possible, rushing and stressing, and probably not giving 100 percent to anything. Or you can choose to prioritize and give the bulk of your time and attention to the things that matter most to you, the things you have been called to by God. That will mean saying no sometimes, both to people you care about and to requests for your time.

Look at your to-do list for the day. Which items are must-dos for keeping your life going (for example, your job or sleeping)? Which items on your list can be cut to make more room for pursuing your dream? Grab a pen and start crossing through the nonessentials. You might be surprised where you can find time to make your dream a priority.

....

....

....

....

....

....

....

41

Value Your Time and Resources

*You must each decide in your heart how much
to give. And don't give reluctantly or in response
to pressure. "For God loves a person who gives
cheerfully." And God will generously provide all you
need. Then you will always have everything you
need and plenty left over to share with others.*

2 CORINTHIANS 9:7–8 NLT

We all have lots to learn to get our dreams off the ground, and that will mean turning to others for advice. Over time, you will become an expert, until, eventually, other dreamers come to you for help.

Friends will want you to help them with their projects, family members will want to show you off, and acquaintances will ask you to connect with their friends. It will be tempting to say yes to every single request, whether you want to or not. You might want to help others, especially when you have received invaluable help yourself, but it's important to remember that saying yes to all of those requests will leave you far less time to do the work of your dream.

God has called you to the work you are doing. That work should not be set aside lightly. Your time and energy are precious, limited resources.

God has called you to the work you are doing right now.

Any request that takes up either should be considered carefully. Here are some questions to ask yourself when faced with such a request:

- Do I feel God calling me to help this person?
- Is this person trying to get free labor that I would normally charge for?
- Is this person serious about her own dream?
- Do I have time or will it mean cancelling on other responsibilities?
- Am I excited about what this person is doing or proposing?
- Do I know anyone else better suited to help this person?

Use wisdom and discernment when giving of yourself. Only say yes when it feels right to you.

42

It's Okay to Say No

Above all, my brothers and sisters, do not swear—
not by heaven or by earth or by anything else.
All you need to say is a simple "Yes" or "No."

JAMES 5:12

It's so much more fun to say yes than no. Saying yes makes people happy and excited. Telling people no often elicits sad and disappointed reactions. Yes is full of energy and anticipation. No is dejection. Yes is a beginning, and no is an ending.

Every time you say yes, you are essentially choosing to say no to something else. Because, unless you have superpowers, it's impossible to be in two places at once or do two very different things at the same time. There are times when you say yes to someone, and because of your choice, you are saying no to your dreams and to the things you want and need. God wants you to help others, but not at the expense of the work He has trusted you with.

> Say yes to the work God has trusted you with.

You can reframe your no. When you say no to a project you aren't connecting with, that is a yes you can say to something you're really excited about. Doesn't it make sense to choose the projects that resonate most with you, knowing your heart will be all in it? When you say no to working late for your job, you can say yes to dinner with your loved ones. When you say no to a collaboration that doesn't help with your dreams, you have freed yourself up to say yes to a partnership that does.

Think through the things you aren't willing to say no to for your life and your dream. Write them below.

....

....

....

....

....

....

....

....

The next time you want to say no to someone, but feel pressure to say yes, try reframing that no as a yes to yourself for something on your list. Does that change how you feel?

43

When Doubt Creeps In

Therefore, my dear brothers and sisters, stand firm. Let nothing move you. Always give yourselves fully to the work of the Lord, because you know that your labor in the Lord is not in vain.

1 CORINTHIANS 15:58

You will have doubts as you pursue your dream. You will have late nights, anxiety, and plenty of thoughts of *What am I even doing?* Everyone does at some point, including people you would never expect to, such as the disciples.

Jesus commissioned His followers to make disciples of everyone they came across, all over the world. Just before that, Matthew writes that the disciples worshipped. Then he adds that some doubted (Matthew 28:16–20). These were the same group of men who had spent three years following Jesus, watching Him perform miracles like raising the dead, casting out demons, walking on water, feeding the masses from fish and bread. You would think they had seen enough proof to forever cast aside their doubts. But even after seeing the resurrected Savior with their own eyes, they still doubted.

> Doubting is natural, but believe that all you're doing is not in vain.

You have far less evidence that your dream will be a success.

If the disciples doubted, it's okay for you to have your moments of doubt too. Of course, those disciples *did* go on to do what Jesus asked, founding the church, sharing the good news, and, in most cases, even dying for their faith. They clearly didn't let their doubts stop them. And you shouldn't either.

Doubting is natural; it's human. Even if you are 100 percent certain that God gave you this dream, you will have doubts. The important thing is that you push through those doubts with faith. Remember that God always comes through, just as He did for the disciples.

Share your doubts and concerns with God. He's always listening.

....

....

....

....

....

....

....

....

44

Give Thanks

*Let us all be thankful that we are a part of an unshakable
Kingdom and offer to God worship that pleases Him and
reflects the awe and reverence we have toward Him.*
HEBREWS 12:28 THE VOICE

Isn't it amazing that God has trusted you with this dream? That
He believes in your abilities to pull it off? That you get to be
the one to experience the joy of walking hand in
hand with God to get it done?

**God's
blessings
will
always
find you.**

Having a dream to motivate and inspire
you is a wonderful blessing, and that dream will
bring many other blessings into your life.

Take a few minutes to think about all of the
blessings God has given you through this dream.
Read each blessing, and tell God thank you for
each one. Continue to add to your list because it
will keep growing. When you are dreaming with
God, His blessings will always find you. As your blessings grow, so
should your gratitude.

45

Your Dreams Will Flourish

*But I am like an olive tree flourishing in the house
of God; I trust in God's unfailing love for ever and
ever. For what you have done I will always praise
you in the presence of your faithful people.*

PSALM 52:8-9

When your dream has come from God, you can trust that He wants you to succeed. He is working right there beside you to amplify your efforts so that you and your dream can thrive and prosper. God has promised that He is working all things for your good, and that is a promise you can trust.

Your part of the deal is to have faith. To trust God completely even when you don't understand why certain things are happening. To love God even when things don't go your way. To praise God even when you fail. To hope in God even when things might seem hopeless. Faith is what He asks for from you, and when you put your complete trust in Him, your faith will flourish.

Can you picture that? Your dreams are a reality, you are flourishing, and you are praising God's name and thanking Him for all that He has done. It's beautiful, isn't it? Think about everything you hope happens with your dream. Consider how you hope to feel, how you want your life to change, and how you want your relationship with God to grow. Then, once your dream has come true, remember how God delivered on your faith.

Part 4: Don't Give Up

Dreams are inherently hopeful. To chase them, you have to truly believe that you have a good shot at making them real. That's why it hurts so much when a dream fails or falls apart on you. It's not just the loss of the dream you mourn when that happens; it's the loss of that hope, the loss of faith in your abilities, your judgment, and, sometimes, in God.

You don't have the advantage of seeing the whole story like God does. He knows that your failed dream is just a few short sentences in the whole story, while you feel like the pain will last forever. When a dream dies, it's important that you remember that the story isn't over yet. You can't possibly know what God has waiting for you in the next paragraph or chapter. This failed dream could be setting you up for the success of an even bigger, better dream that God will be sending your way. God could just be waiting for the right moment to resurrect this dream in His perfect timing. Or, as much as you wanted it to be, this dream may not have come from God at all, which is why it failed.

When you get to the very end of your story, those moments of failure and mourning and frustration will likely make a lot more sense. Until then, you can lean on your faith in God and never give up on working to make the dreams He has given you come true.

46

When Dreams Fail

Blessed is the one whom God corrects; so do not despise the discipline of the Almighty. For he wounds, but he also binds up; he injures, but his hands also heal.

JOB 5:17–18

Sometimes dreams fall apart. It's okay (and perfectly normal) to feel devastated, betrayed, sad, and angry. You might be angry at yourself, or others, or even at God. Fortunately, God is big enough to withstand a little anger. He'll be right there waiting when the anger ebbs and you realize just how much

> **God is always ready to listen to your heart.**

you need Him. When your charged emotions start to settle, use this prayer and tell God how you feel. He knows you're hurting and disappointed that a dream failed, and He's ready to listen.

Lord,

I am devastated. My dream has shattered into pieces too small for me to put back together. All of my hope and excitement feels wasted in this moment. I know that I did everything I could to get this thing off the ground, but it really hurts that my best wasn't good enough.

I don't know what to do now. Should I give up? I thought that You gave me this dream. But maybe You didn't. Maybe this is something I cooked up in my head, and I need to let it go. Lord, please fill me with peace at the thought of stepping away if that's what's best. I don't want to desire what You don't want for me.

If You did give me this dream, please show me the next steps. Make the way forward clear, even if the way forward is just to wait and heal for now. I trust You. I have faith that You will resurrect this dream if it's part of Your plan and, if not, that You will lead me to something far better.

In the meantime, please comfort and heal me. Help me to see all of the good that is still present, and help the grief to pass.

In Jesus' name, amen.

47

When Your Plans Fall Apart

When I said, "My foot is slipping," your unfailing love, LORD, supported me. When anxiety was great within me, your consolation brought me joy.

PSALM 94:18–19

It's never easy when something that you poured your heart into fails. It hurts. On top of feeling disappointed and sad, failure is usually accompanied by shame and embarrassment. It can make you lose faith in your abilities and your vision, afraid to try again, afraid to trust. All of that together is a toxic recipe for turning away from God.

> God has overcome the world, and He is with you.

It's important to remember that God promises many times throughout the Bible that you will have troubles. You were never promised prosperity and an easy road. The world is sometimes a difficult place to be, but God has overcome the world. This pain, as terrible and heavy as it may feel right now, will not last forever. There are some things you can do to help you heal.

- Give control to God and then do your best to let it go. He's got this.
- Take time to grieve. Let yourself feel your feelings. Take however long you need to work through all of your emotions. After all, Jesus wept too.
- Lean on your people. Your community of family, friends, and fellow dreamers will be there for you. Be open about what you are dealing with so that they can walk alongside you and help support you.
- Realign your desires with God's desires for you. It's not like life comes with a step-by-step manual for your particular journey, but you do have a guidebook. Crack open your Bible, and make sure that the dream you've been chasing lines up with God's Word. If it doesn't, depending on what your dream was, it's time to go back to your life coach, your therapist, your mentor, or perhaps even back to the drawing board.
- When you're ready, start dreaming again, involving God in every step along the way. His dreams are waiting for you, full of passion and purpose.

48

Get Back Up

Even youths grow tired and weary, and young
men stumble and fall; but those who hope in
the LORD will renew their strength. They will
soar on wings like eagles; they will run and not
grow weary, they will walk and not be faint.
ISAIAH 40:30–31

You might fall down, but you don't have to stay down. If your hope is placed firmly in God, you will find the strength in Him to get back up. God doesn't want you to live life beaten, demoralized, and hating yourself. He loves you, and He wants you to love yourself. He has faith in you and wants you to have faith in Him. He has planned good things for your life, so you can trust Him when you're down.

> The world needs you and your dreams because you make a difference.

Have you ever fallen flat on your face? Did it feel like things would never be good again? Maybe you've wondered if things were ever good to begin with. But those thoughts are not based in truth. If you flip back through this book, you'll see where you've noted ways that God has blessed you, where He's made previous dreams come true, and how He's brought the people you've needed into your life. He has always been working for you, always loving you.

Being knocked down hurts, so take the time you need to heal, but don't stay down so long that you begin to believe that you belong there. You don't. You belong out there in the world making a difference. Remind yourself of that, multiple times a day if you need to. It might help to create a mantra you can say to yourself when you need that reminder. Something like, "I've been down, but I'm never out with God." Or "I learn every time I fall, and I get back up stronger than ever." Use these examples to create a mantra that works for you. Write your mantra here so you can refer to it as needed.

....

....

....

....

....

....

....

....

....

....

....

....

....

49

Ask for Help

I rise before dawn and cry for help;
I have put my hope in your word.

PSALM 119:147

When we mess up or fail, our natural inclination is to try to hide our mistakes and fix the issues ourselves. This is nothing new. From the time Adam and Eve hid from God in the Garden of Eden, we've been trying to hide our messes from God. But it wasn't a good plan for Adam and Eve, and it isn't a good plan now. Hiding a mess doesn't make it go away, and shouldering a crushing burden alone will eventually crush you.

God is ready to provide you with all you need to keep going.

Make no mistake, God can clearly see that mess you're trying to hide. You aren't fooling Him. But in hiding and turning away from Him, you're only hurting yourself more. God wants you to turn to Him for help when you need it (and even when you don't!). He's ready to make things happen on your behalf, to provide comfort and healing, or to inspire you with new dreams. All you have to do is ask.

It isn't just God that you hide from, though, is it? You try to hide your missteps from people too, even from your loved ones. Maybe you've closed yourself off from the people who love you most and want to help you because you're embarrassed or ashamed. But don't forget the truth that everyone fails. Those who sincerely love you will understand, and they will be ready to support you and help you however they can.

What are some problems you are facing right now? How can you ask for help from God and from those who love you?

....

....

....

....

....

....

....

....

....

....

50

God Will Catch You

*The steps of a good man are ordered by the LORD, and He
delights in his way. Though he fall, he shall not be utterly
cast down; for the LORD upholds him with His hand.*

PSALM 37:23-24 NKJV

One of God's promises to you is that He will catch you when you
fall. That's not to say that you won't experience falling, because
you will. But He will catch you before you hit
the bottom. When you find yourself without
solid footing, when you feel as though you're in
a free fall, call to God, and He will reach out
His hand for you. Use this prayer as a way to
start the conversation with Him.

**God will
always
catch you**

Yahweh,

*I feel like I'm stuck in an endless free fall. Every time I
think I'm going to catch myself, something else knocks me off
my feet. It's just been one issue after another. I believe so much
in this dream, but it seems like I'm the only one who sees the
potential and why it's worth pursuing.*

*I desperately need a break. I need an easy week, a chance
to catch my breath and regroup. I'd even take a single day
without problems. I know, Lord, that You are the only One
who can give me that break. Please, I need You to catch me,*

to pull me out of free fall and give me a little time on the solid foundation of Your hand.

I know I've made mistakes. Things haven't worked out the way I'd hoped. The support I was expecting has evaporated. I can't turn this around on my own. If this is the dream You planned for me, I need You to build a bridge across the chasm stretching out before me. You're the only One who can. Even if You don't, I trust You to pick me up and put me back on the right path.

In Jesus' name, amen.

51

Trust in God

*Many put their hope in chariots, others in horses, but we place
our trust in the name of the Eternal One, our True God.*
PSALM 20:7 THE VOICE

You've probably heard about a "sure thing" when it comes to getting rich, becoming successful, or achieving your dreams. If you
just take this course, invest in this workshop or coaching, buy in for
exclusive stock tips, or attend this conference, then you, too, can
become as successful and wealthy as all of the people selling all this
stuff. When your dreams have come to a grinding
halt, that *stuff* looks especially appealing.

**You can
put your
trust in
God.**

Who doesn't want concrete answers, steps
that, if taken correctly, will lead to a predictable,
successful outcome? But that's just not how life
works. Life is unpredictable and always has been.
God is and always will be the only constant, the
only place worth putting your trust. When you
put your trust in those "sure things," you are taking your trust
away from God.

The Bible is full of examples of other believers who struggled
to trust God.

- Eve ate the fruit (Genesis 3:6).
- Abraham laughed (Genesis 17:4–17).

- Sarah laughed too (Genesis 18:9–15).
- Lot's wife looked back (Genesis 19:17–26).
- Job's wife left her husband in the ash heap (Job 2:9).
- Jonah ran away from God (Jonah 1:1–3).
- Thomas doubted (John 20:25).

If you find yourself tempted to put your trust in something earthly to make your dreams come true, know that you aren't the first. Learn from those Bible stories. It's not too late to put your trust back where it belongs—in God. He's waiting for you.

52

Grief Will Not Last Forever

"Truly, truly, I say to you, you will weep and lament, but the world will rejoice. You will be sorrowful, but your sorrow will turn into joy."

JOHN 16:20 ESV

There is no right or wrong way to grieve, so long as you actually let yourself feel the sadness and loss that you have experienced. Processing and dealing with your feelings is the healthiest thing you can do, even if it means a lot of tears over pints of ice cream or on a therapist's couch. The worst thing you can do when a dream falls apart is to press on as if that loss didn't affect you. (If the loss of a dream truly doesn't make you feel anything, then it probably wasn't a dream you should have been pursuing!) Dreams require passion and dedication and vision. So, it's going to hurt when your plans and work don't pan out the way you hoped.

> It's okay to grieve. Know that you will heal.

The good news is that no grief lasts forever. That doesn't mean that you won't still wish that your dream had worked out or that you won't think about it sometimes, but the pain of losing it will lessen little by little until it no longer hurts to remember the work you put into it. Lean on God. Lament. Heal. Then be ready to dream again.

Think back to other times when you have lost something or someone dear to you. How long did it take you to feel better? What helped you the most during that grieving period?

53

Cling to Hope

As for me, I will always have hope; I
will praise you more and more.

PSALM 71:14

God will never leave you alone, will never, ever abandon you. Even when life feels dark or too challenging or actually impossible, God is always there, reaching out to you to bring you through it. Part of what it means to be a Christian is to trust that even when it seems hopeless, there will always be hope to cling to in Jesus.

You won't always understand why things fall apart or why your dreams don't work out. Heartbreak usually doesn't make sense. But when it happens, you are so blessed to be able to rest and heal in God. You might not notice them right away through the haze of your grief, but God has filled your life with little reminders of the hope you have in Him. These good things are there to encourage you and keep you going until things feel better.

God sends reminders for you to keep your hope alive.

What gives you hope on your darkest days? A morning spent in quiet time with God? Time spent with loved ones? There are no wrong answers. Next time you need a dose of hope, remember your answers, and when you're ready, get up and keep fighting for your dreams.

54

When You Face Rejection

*Jesus said to them, "Have you never read in
the Scriptures: 'The stone the builders rejected
has become the cornerstone; the Lord has done
this, and it is marvelous in our eyes'?"*

MATTHEW 21:42

No one likes to be rejected or laughed at. The fear of rejection alone is enough to keep most dreamers from becoming doers. However, no rejection can stand when God enters into the equation. You'll be told no a lot in this life. It's okay to be disappointed by that; just remember that when you are dreaming with God, all of those nos are for a reason. They are not the path you need to be on or the people you need to be working with (either at the time or ever). Remember that by shifting your perspective a little, you can see a rejection as a redirection, as God leading you toward the yeses that will make a way for your dreams. When you receive a rejection, use this prayer as a way of starting a conversation with God about it.

> God can turn your rejection into your growth.

Heavenly Father,

I feel like all I hear lately is no. It's so disheartening having my ideas and plans belittled or overlooked. It hurts when people don't get it or, even worse, just don't want it. I want people to take me and this dream seriously.

I have faith that You gave me this particular dream for a reason. I'm going to keep working, no matter how many nos I hear. I know that I can count on You to turn those nos into yeses at the right time. When that happens, everyone who has followed me on this journey will see how powerful and good You are.

Until that day, Lord, please soothe my bruised heart and ego. Help this rejection mold me to become humbler, more patient, and more like You. Inspire me to keep improving my plans. Grant me the wisdom to see which feedback will make a difference and which to ignore. Please keep working in me to keep me from becoming bitter, to keep my heart soft and optimistic.

In Jesus' name, amen.

55

The Comparison Trap

Do not let your heart envy sinners, but always be
zealous for the fear of the LORD. There is surely a
future hope for you, and your hope will not be cut off.
PROVERBS 23:17–19

There's a saying that "comparison is the thief of joy." When you spend your time focused on what others have or what they are accomplishing, it often distracts you from what you have and what you are doing. None of us can possibly know what others are going through behind the scenes. It may look like they have it all together, but that doesn't mean they actually do. And, even if they do have it all together, they are living out the dreams and plans God has given *them*. As good as they may look, the simple truth is that those dreams and plans aren't yours.

> Go to God for truth, then listen to your heart.

Comparison is at its height thanks to the internet. Between blogs, TED talks, podcasts, and social media, you have a myriad of windows to peek through to see other people's highlight reels. Does anyone really put her worst moments, his secret shame, their traumatic failures up on the internet somewhere for everyone to gawk at? Mostly likely not. If choosing what you share, you probably intentionally upload images, stories, recordings, and writings that showcase the best of your life.

The internet, as essential as it is, is not a place to go for the truth. If you want to turn off the comparison and focus on where you have been called, to your own dreams, you need to spend less time on the internet and more time with God.

What is your worst comparison trap on the internet? Why do you think that particular source of content gets under your skin so easily?

....

....

....

....

....

....

....

....

....

56

Getting Unstuck

He brought me out into a spacious place; he
rescued me because he delighted in me.

PSALM 18:19

Dreams get derailed in a lot of ways, but one of the most common is that you get stuck. Have you encountered a roadblock you can't get around? Have you forgotten why you started down the path to this dream? Or maybe you've taken on too much and your dream gets put on the back burner. This stuck feeling may happen more than once as you pursue your dream, so when you feel it, try one of these strategies to get unstuck.

Taking care of yourself is vital for your dreams.

- Take a break. Don't think about your issue for at least three days. Do other things, and let your subconscious work on the problem without you.
- Switch your focus. Choose to work on a different part of your dream, preferably something that makes you feel inspired. It will give you a much-needed change of perspective.
- Bust open your routine. Go work in the park or a coffee shop you've never been to before. Hike up to a pretty spot or take a walk on the beach. A new view can sometimes make all the difference.

- Try something new. Focus on learning a new skill (preferably one that will help with your dream). Learning changes the physical structure of the brain and may shake loose a solution you hadn't considered yet.
- Call in your community. Talk to your creative community or loved ones about why you feel stuck. They may have good advice or see something you've missed.
- Take care of yourself. Get some extra sleep, go for a long walk, read a good book. Do whatever you feel your mind and body need to recharge. None of us thinks best when we are running on fumes. A little care may be just what you need.

57

Take Time to Rest

The LORD is my shepherd, I lack nothing. He
makes me lie down in green pastures, he leads
me beside quiet waters, he refreshes my soul.
PSALM 23:1–3

When life blocks your plans, or puts your dreams on hold, it may just be a pause before the action picks back up. Instead of spinning your wheels fretting, take the time to rest and prepare yourself for what's to come. Say this prayer, telling God how you're feeling about the lack of forward motion and asking Him to help you learn to rest when that is what is needed most.

> It's okay to pause your dreams so you can rest.

Father God,

Everything is at a standstill right now. I'm doing my best not to let my anxious fears run away with me, but I keep imagining the worst. This may be the end of the road for this dream. Only You know that for sure. I'm doing my best to remember that You are in control and, more importantly, I want You to be. Your way is always better than my way.

God, please help me to use this time wisely. Grant me Your peace to quiet my fears and Your confidence to squash my anxiety. Help me to settle into a rhythm of rest for my body, mind, and soul. I've been going at such a breakneck pace for so long, it almost feels like I've forgotten how to go slowly. Please help me remember.

You've brought so many amazing people into my life. Whom should I connect with right now? Please guide me as I plan my schedule, help me to feel out how I should be spending my time intuitively. I want to find ways to quiet my racing mind, ways to prioritize soothing my soul through time with You. Help me connect to my body and what it needs to be rested and strong and prepared for whatever You have planned for me next.

In Your Son's name, amen.

58

You Will Fail

*For all have sinned and fall short of the glory
of God, and are justified by his grace as a gift,
through the redemption that is in Christ Jesus.*

ROMANS 3:23-24 ESV

ailure is a part of life. Without failure, you wouldn't learn and
grow and discover new things about yourself as easily or at
all. Hitting a wall forces you to learn how to think creatively to
solve problems. Flopping teaches you humility. Getting knocked
down teaches you how to find the strength to get
back up. Being down forces you to look up,
where you find God waiting for you. Failure
teaches you far more than success ever will.
When you accept that failure is a necessary
part of life, it won't feel so scary anymore.

**God is
waiting for
you to look
up to Him.**

There is something freeing in acknowl-
edging that some failure is inevitable. It goes
hand in hand with taking risks, pushing bound-
aries, and trying new things. Dreamers are the ones who blaze
new trails, so of course you're going to fail. You can't forge a path
through unexplored territory without falling into a few holes or
encountering the unexpected. But with every failure, you will learn
a little more, so that next time, you'll have a better idea of what to

do. And eventually, you'll have earned the wisdom that you need to succeed.

Remember, God is with you in failure, just as He is with you in success. When failure feels scary or overwhelming, lean on Him to help you through.

Think back to other times when you've failed. What did you learn? How did those failures change you for the better?

....

....

....

....

....

....

....

....

59

Learn from Your Failure

Count it all joy, my brothers, when you meet
trials of various kinds, for you know that the
testing of your faith produces steadfastness. And
let steadfastness have its full effect, that you may
be perfect and complete, lacking in nothing.

JAMES 1:2–4 ESV

Life would certainly be easier without failure. When you are the one in the midst of failing, especially if it's because of circumstances outside of your control, it's easy to feel upset and resentful about it. And it can be tempting to be angry at God for letting you fail. But God doesn't let you fail to punish you. He lets you fail because failure refines you, helps you become more fully who you are meant to be, and draws you closer to Him. Failure is a gift.

Failure can be used as a gift.

Failure drives innovation. For every successful person out there, there is a list of failures a mile long behind her. Some of the failures are her fault, and others are not; but without all of those failures, big and small, she wouldn't be where she is today.

Just look at David. He was a man after God's own heart, yet he failed numerous times. He was faithless at times, such as when he ordered a census in direct opposition to God's orders (2 Samuel 24:1–15). His failure resulted in a plague. He coveted his beautiful neighbor, Bathsheba, slept with her, and then orchestrated her husband's death to preserve his reputation (2 Samuel 11:1–17). When confronted with his failures, David repented. He learned from what he had done wrong and did his best not to repeat those failures again. You can do the same thing.

Think of your most recent failure. What is it teaching you? How can you make it into something beautiful as you move forward?

....

....

....

....

....

....

....

....

....

60

Trust the Dream Placed in Your Heart

I am sure of this, that he who began a good work in you
will bring it to completion at the day of Jesus Christ.
PHILIPPIANS 1:6 ESV

Have you ever felt like all hope is lost, but you still can't shake the feeling that your dream is still viable? Don't discount that feeling because God is the Author of hope. If He's kindled that hope in your heart, it's for a good reason. It might be that your dream will be resurrected. Or that this dream will give way to an even bigger dream. Whatever the reason, trust that feeling. Trust the truth that God has placed in your heart. Use this prayer as a way to start a conversation with Him.

> **God kindles your hope for a purpose.**

Yahweh,
I feel confused and lost right now. Everything is just such a mess! I want to be productive and come up with new plans and find a way to fix this dream, but I am stumped. This isn't a problem that I can fix. It's only something that You can fix.
I trust that this dream is a dream that You placed in my heart, and I'm not willing to give up on it so easily. I know

that since this dream came from You, You will see it through. I know that Your time line and my time line aren't usually the same. I want everything urgently, quickly, while You are patient, biding Your time until the perfect moment. I can wait patiently with You because I have faith in You and I have faith in this dream.

That's not to say that I'll be good at waiting. I'm sure I'll have moments—maybe even days—of impatience. I'll feel grumpy and frustrated and wish things were moving faster. Please keep filling my well of patience. Please keep soothing my racing mind and reminding me that You are right here with me. I need You with me to keep up the vigil. I can do it as long as You are here.

In Jesus' name, amen.

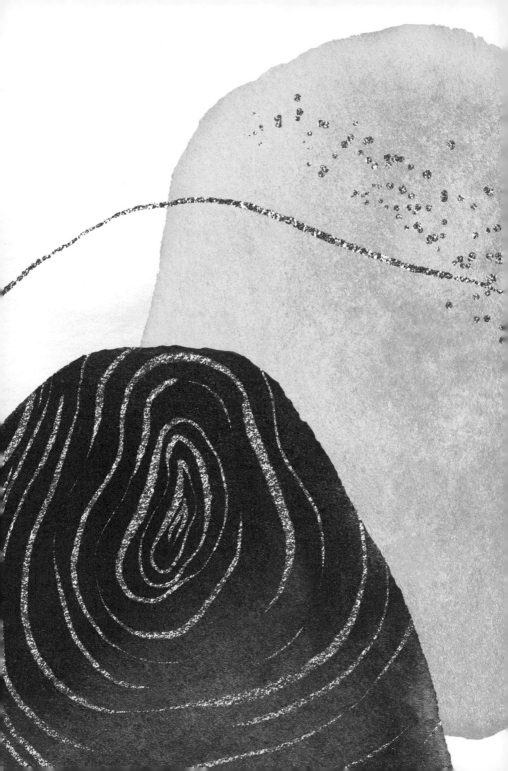

Part 5: Keep It Up

It would be great if all of your dreams could be accomplished quickly and easily. While some dreams are like that, most aren't. Many dreams take years or even lifetimes to come to fruition. And so many of your dreams aren't really one-and-done situations. Most dreams involve starting something and then continuing to do that thing successfully for a long time.

If your dream is to be a successful writer and you publish your first book, technically, you accomplished your dream. But it's unlikely that you would say your dream was done. You would probably want to write and publish more books, right? And have them sell well? If your dream is to open a bakery, the dream isn't over when you open the doors for the first time. You'll desire to continue to run the bakery and have it be profitable, right?

Most of your dreams are for the long haul. You need stamina, persistence, and faith to keep going. Knowing that you have God right there, working with you, is so comforting. He isn't going to leave you to dream alone, no matter how long your dreams last. He'll be right beside you during the early mornings and all through the late nights, during bad months and months that outstrip even your wildest expectations. He'll be with you when you consider giving up and when you feel inspired to dream even bigger.

God is not just a part of your dreams; He is your dreams. He is the love, the forgiveness, and the hope that ultimately inspires you to go out and change the world for the better. You can keep going because you have Him.

61

Pace Yourself

*Let us not grow weary of doing good, for in due
season we will reap, if we do not give up.*

GALATIANS 6:9 ESV

Making a dream come true takes dedication, effort, and time.
There's only so long you can sprint before you will lose steam
entirely. When you feel tired, you lose motivation, and when you
lose motivation, you are far more likely to give up. You have to pace
yourself if you want to go the distance.

You can't serve God if you are too worn
out to get any work done. When you respect
your limitations and honor the needs of
your body, you'll have the energy and
bandwidth to step up and embrace the
challenges God has waiting for you. You
want to keep pace with God, running stead-
ily beside Him and His plans for your life, not
falling behind or sprinting out ahead of Him.

> **Some dreams
> are more like
> a marathon
> than a sprint.
> Remember to
> pace yourself.**

When you are deeply enthusiastic about what you are doing,
pacing yourself can be challenging. But there are ways to do it!

- Plan your day with intention. Go over your schedule with
  God each morning. Listen for His direction.

- Say no and stick to it. Save your yeses for things that really matter.
- Prioritize your dream. This dream is yours. No one else will put it first, so you have to.
- Feel your feelings. Feel and process your emotions as they come up so you can truly move on, and they won't pop up to trip you up later.
- Schedule time for rest. Put caring for yourself on your calendar. Family meals, a good night's sleep, and exercise will keep your mind sharp and your spirits high.
- Don't rush. There are very few decisions that truly must be made on the spot. You have time to think it over.

62

Find Your Groove

*"Six days you shall work, but on the seventh day you
shall rest. In plowing time and in harvest you shall rest."*

EXODUS 34:21 ESV

Sometimes less truly is more. You know that you think better, problem solve more efficiently, and are able to relax and listen more easily when you are well rested, right? But when you are chasing a dream that matters deeply to you, it can feel like there isn't time for rest. But the work that you do when you are sleep-deprived and over-scheduled won't be your best. And this dream of your heart deserves your very best.

Embrace a time of rest.

As a society, we have elevated busyness into high art. It's less about how much quality work we produce and more about how many things we have to do. But the two don't actually go hand in hand. You can be incredibly busy with a neatly checked off to-do list a mile long and still not have done anything worthwhile. Resting is so vital that God included it in His Word.

Embrace a day of rest.

- Take a nap.
- Go for a leisurely stroll.
- Turn off your phone.
- Take another nap.

- Read a fun book.
- Do a puzzle.
- Watch your favorite movie.
- Go to bed early.

None of us wants to be perceived as lazy—we all know what Scripture says about that!—but, all too often, we swing too far in the other direction, which isn't any better. One of the most frequently repeated commands in the Old Testament is to honor the Sabbath. Scripture is quite clear about your need for rest to renew your heart, your mind, and your faith in worship, regardless of how much work you have left to do. There is a happy medium between being lazy and being a workaholic, and that's the well-rested—but focused—space you need to live in.

63

Be Diligent

Lazy people want much but get little, but
those who work hard will prosper.

PROVERBS 13:4 NLT

The Bible talks a lot about hard work, diligence, and perseverance, so we know that those things are important when it comes to doing God's work. The dreamers who succeed are all incredibly hard workers. But you must also acknowledge that there will be times when that isn't enough, when only divine intervention from God can make your dreams work. In those times, you must be diligent in turning to God and asking for help. When you don't want to give up on your dream but you feel unsure of how best to proceed, use this prayer and talk to God. Ask Him for guidance and assurance.

God has wondrous plans for you.

Lord,
My dream is at a standstill. I've done everything I can think of and exhausted every resource I have available to me. I've followed the plans I worked through with You, but this is beyond my control. I need You to make this happen. I need a miracle.
I've never seen water turned into wine or anyone walking on water, but I don't need to see those miracles to believe in

them and find hope in them. Just reading the stories of how they happened is enough for me. I have absolute faith that You still perform miracles today. I cannot achieve this dream without You.

I have worked so hard and handled every detail with painstaking attention. I am failing, but anyone can see that it is not for a lack of effort. When You step in to save the day, it will be clear just who is in control. I will shout praises to Your name and point others to Your power and goodness in my life regardless of what happens with my dream. I trust that You have bigger plans for this dream than I do and that You have something wondrous planned for this moment too. I can't wait to see it in action.

In Jesus' name, amen.

64

Celebrate Successes and Share Failures

Rejoice with those who rejoice; mourn
with those who mourn.

ROMANS 12:15

Throw yourself a party! Invite your friends, blow up balloons, buy a funfetti cake. It's time to raise a toast to just how far you've come. Most dreams don't happen overnight. They take time, and much of that work is done in fits and starts. So when you reach a milestone or accomplish something big on the road to your dreams, it's important to take the time to celebrate that!

> God brings people into your life for a reason.

Bring your community in to acknowledge all of the work that has been completed. It will help keep you motivated and inspired, and it will also likely motivate other dreamers who are just starting out or might be in a bit of a funk.

What have you already accomplished that deserves a slice of celebratory cake?

....

....

Likewise, bring your community in when things feel decidedly less celebratory. When you fail spectacularly or learn an important lesson the hard way, you don't have to suffer through it alone. Let your friends grieve with you when a door closes and can't be opened again. Let your people pick you up and dust you off when you fall. Let them love you when you are hurting.

God brought together this community around you to support you and love you. You don't have to fear judgment or shame from them. Share what you did and didn't do right to get their advice and perspectives. And, even more importantly, share what you have learned. You never know who in your circle may need that lesson for their own dreams.

What lessons have you already learned by failing?

....

....

....

....

65

Stay Inspired

Therefore we do not lose heart. Even though our outward man is perishing, yet the inward man is being renewed day by day.

2 CORINTHIANS 4:16 NKJV

There will be days when your dream doesn't seem very dreamy. You will lose motivation or find yourself stumped by a problem that you just can't seem to get around. You will have times when you will feel uninspired. This happens to everyone eventually. The good news is that there are things you can do to relight that fire inside of you for your dream.

Focus on what brings you to life and inspires you.

- Pray and ask God for His inspiration. He will renew you.
- Make a vision board for your dream, using pictures from magazines or your own work. Place it somewhere you see often. Update the board often.
- Spend some time doing things that inspire you—go to a museum or art gallery, get tickets to a concert, or attend a play.
- Ask your community for inspiring book recommendations— read as many as you can.

- Schedule time to catch up with your most inspiring friends. Their enthusiasm can be contagious.
- Get back to the goals you created for your dream previously in this book. They might need to be updated. Write out why you are pursuing this dream over others, why this dream matters to you, and why this work is worth doing. Your goals should be motivating. If they aren't, rework them.
- Take a break and focus on something else for a week or two (or even a weekend if your time line is tight!). Clean out your garage, weed your flower beds, or deep clean your house. While you handle those physical tasks, your subconscious will keep working on your dream, and you'll get back to work with new ideas already formed and waiting for you.

66

Burnout Is Real

*But he himself went a day's journey into the wilderness
and came and sat down under a broom tree. And he asked
that he might die, saying, "It is enough; now, O LORD,
take away my life, for I am no better than my fathers."*

1 KINGS 19:4 ESV

Elijah was a busy guy. On a single, quite notable day, he orchestrated the execution of 450 prophets of Baal and then climbed to the top of a mountain to pray for rain. Once God granted his request, he ran miles and miles to the palace of Queen Jezebel, only to find Jezebel unimpressed by God's power. Then, she threatened his life. Suffice it to say, Elijah lost it. He ran out into the desert and asked God to kill him.

God cares for you.

When you think about it, it's no wonder that Elijah said, "It is enough." He had worked without ceasing, completing difficult task after task, only to find that his work was for nothing . . . or at least that's how it seemed to him then.

Elijah had hit his limit. He was exhausted, hungry, thirsty, and just plain done. He had burned out. As a result, he wasn't able to think clearly at all. If he had, he would have realized that Jezebel didn't have the power to kill him. It was an empty threat. Instead, he threw an epic tantrum.

God could have rebuked Elijah, but He didn't. Instead, God cared for him tenderly. He sent an angel to watch over Elijah, shielding him from harm as he recuperated. Once his body had recovered, Elijah's perspective shifted and his clarity returned. His faith was renewed, and he was ready to start solving problems with God again.

Has this ever happened to you? What are some signs that help you realize that you are burning out? What are some actions you can take to protect yourself when you feel burnout coming?

....

....

....

....

....

....

....

....

....

....

....

....

67

Take Care of Yourself

And he lay down and slept under a broom tree. And behold, an angel touched him and said to him, "Arise and eat." And he looked, and behold, there was at his head a cake baked on hot stones and a jar of water. And he ate and drank and lay down again. And the angel of the LORD came again a second time and touched him and said, "Arise and eat, for the journey is too great for you." And he arose and ate and drank, and went in the strength of that food forty days and forty nights.

1 KINGS 19:5–8 ESV

God created your mind and body to work in harmony with one another. When your body is unwell, your mind won't work as effectively, and when your mind is troubled, your body will feel the effects. Scripture focuses so often on your spiritual wellness, but sometimes the answer is physical. The story of Elijah is a perfect example of that.

> Take care of your whole body—body, mind, and soul.

When Elijah arrived in the desert, he was completely overwrought. The first thing God did was help Elijah sleep deeply. Then, He sent an angel to bring Elijah food and water. Then He helped him sleep some *more*. And sent *more* food and drink. God knew that what

Elijah needed was physical comfort, so He tended to his needs, and He didn't rush Elijah through recovery.

When you find yourself frazzled, short-tempered, and exhausted, the solution is simple. Rest. Drink water. Eat nourishing food. Take care of your body, and your mind and optimistic attitude will be taken care of too. Say this prayer, and talk to God about ways He can help you make sure you are taking care of yourself.

Yahweh,

I know that rest is important, but, somehow, I always seem to think it's important for everyone except me. So many people depend on me. I have so many responsibilities. Taking care of myself inevitably falls to the bottom of the list. Thank You for the story of Elijah, a reminder of how important it is to make caring for my body a priority. Please keep reminding me. Help me to return to this story when I feel overwhelmed like Elijah did.

In Jesus' name, amen.

68

Leave Room for Rest and Comfort

*Yes, my soul, find rest in God; my hope comes
from him. Truly he is my rock and my salvation;
he is my fortress, I will not be shaken.*

PSALM 62:5–6

If you want your dream to go the distance, you have to be intentional about rest. Even God took a day of rest when He created literally everything, so that tells you how important it is to build time to care for yourself into your busy schedule.

Self-care isn't just bubble baths and face masks (although those are fun too!); taking care of yourself means connecting with God every day, dealing with your emotions in healthy ways, listening to and honoring the needs of your body, and taking time for fun and connection with those dearest to you. No matter how much you love what you are working on, there can be too much of a good thing.

> Be intentional about self-care and rest.

If you are in need of a break, add some of these restful forms of self-care to your planner.

- Daily quiet time with your Bible, an inspiring devotional, and God.
- Write out your feelings in a journal.
- Clear your mind, and enjoy quiet time with meditation, yoga, or a bubble bath.
- Get outside and spend time in nature.
- Move your body. Go for a walk, dance in the living room, or take a fun exercise class.
- Grab a long lunch with your favorite friends and laugh until your sides hurt.
- Get eight hours of sleep a night, or, if you can't, take naps.
- Reread your favorite book or a fun, new release.
- Get away for the weekend.
- Indulge in nourishing foods that give you energy.
- Pray and ask God for His peace and rest.

69

Build Community

*Bear one another's burdens, and so
fulfill the law of Christ.*

GALATIANS 6:2 ESV

Dreamers need other dreamers. You need people who understand what it means to have deep faith and take big risks for your dreams. You need their encouragement, support, and advice. You need people who will see the potential in your dreams and join you in making them real. You need one another. Start praying today to find your people. Use this prayer as a way to start the communication with God about helping you find your creative community of dreamers.

> **Dreamers need other dreamers.**

Father God,

I know that You and I working together can make this dream happen, but I also know that You want us to live in community. So, I'm praying that You will help me find my community. Please bring the right people into my life. Send me people who will challenge my plans, reveal their weaknesses, and help me make my dream stronger. Nudge me to meet the people who will inspire me to work harder and smarter. Help me have honest conversations with my friends, family, and neighbors so I can find the people who dream as big as

I do—so we can keep one another inspired and encouraged. Bring me people after Your heart whose faith will bolster my own.

Help me to identify the people in my life who will tear me down, make me doubt myself and You, and keep me living small when I could be living so big by following these dreams You have given me. I don't want to miss out on that big life. I don't want to miss out on the relationships You want me to have because I'm clinging to the wrong ones. Give me the wisdom to see which people are my people and the courage to let go of the people who aren't.

In Your Son's name, amen.

70

Dream Together

As iron sharpens iron, so one person sharpens another.
PROVERBS 27:17

All of our individual dreams are great, but there are so many opportunities for us to combine our dreams together to create something even bigger and more impactful. Your dream plus your best friend's or cousin's or neighbor's dream combined may take you both so much further than just yours alone ever could.

> God has placed creative, talented, and inspiring people in your life for a purpose.

God has filled your life with amazing people for a reason. He wants you to live and work and dream together to help one another and make this world better for everyone. Think about the dreams your friends and family are pursuing.

Is there any way that one of their dreams could work with yours?

....

....

....

....

....

Maybe your dream doesn't quite go with the dreams others are pursuing. But that shouldn't stop you.

Is there anything you could be doing to help one of your people with her dream? Do you have skills or connections or experience that could make things easier for her?

....

....

....

....

....

....

....

Offer yourself to your people. You never know how God might be planning to use you in their stories. Be their biggest dream supporter. Be their fiercest prayer warrior. Be their biggest celebrator. Let God multiply your work for them and their work for you in big ways when you are there for each other.

71

Get Help When You Need It

Don't think you are better than you really are. Be honest in your evaluation of yourselves, measuring yourselves by the faith God has given us.

ROMANS 12:3 NLT

Everyone has areas where they excel and areas where they struggle. There is no shame in not being good at everything. There's a reason that God doesn't make you good at everything, and it's not because He *couldn't* do that.

God wants to do this dream with you. He wants you to lean on Him, to ask Him for His help, and accept that He can do things that you just can't. But God also uses your weaknesses to bring the right people in to help you. In an ideal world, you would spend all of your time doing what you're great at and enjoy doing. But more than likely, you are spending most of your time doing things that you aren't good at just to have the chance to do what you love for a very small portion of time.

> Be honest with yourself about when you need a little extra help.

If you want to be a singer, you will have to schedule studio and rehearsal space, write songs, find musicians and producers, sign contracts, and book gigs. None of that is singing. Either you can spend way too much of your time doing all of that stuff—and likely not doing it all that well—or you can ask for help. A great manager will handle the business side of things, giving you time to sing. Doesn't that sound better?

You already know which parts of your dream you want to do. What parts do you struggle with? List them here and then start praying for God to bring the right helpers to support you.

....

....

....

....

....

....

....

....

....

....

....

....

....

12

When It Seems Like No One Sees Your Hard Work

[Hagar] called the name of the LORD who spoke to her, "You are a God of seeing," for she said, "Truly here I have seen him who looks after me."

GENESIS 16:13 ESV

Going full steam after the dream of your heart takes dedication, hard work, perseverance, and then more hard work for good measure. When you are working that hard for weeks, months, or maybe even years, it only makes sense that a time will come when you feel unappreciated.

Some dreams require you to gather up lots of people to help you, to be on your team, and to help you shoulder the workload. No one will care or work as hard as you do, of course, because it is *your* dream, but the people on your team will care a lot. They will work hard with you.

> God is with you for every single step of your dream.

But other dreams require you to work alone. There won't be a team, just you, working on long nights and weekends and on holidays and vacations. Most of the time the work won't feel like work. But sometimes the burden of all the planning and all the work resting only on your shoulders can feel awfully heavy. When your friends and family members have no idea just how much you are doing, working on your dream can feel less invigorating and a lot lonelier.

In those moments, there are a few verses you can read to remind you that you are never alone. God is always there for every minute you put in working toward your dream. He sees all that you do, and He appreciates your faith and obedience to His calling.

- Joshua 1:9
- Isaiah 41:10
- Zephaniah 3:17
- Matthew 28:20
- Psalm 23:4
- Philippians 4:13
- Psalm 73:26

13

Have Confidence in God's Plans for You

"Even if I am making bold claims about Myself—who I am, what I have come to do—I am speaking the truth."
JOHN 8:14 THE VOICE

When your dreams and plans come from God, you can be certain that they will eventually happen. Your dreams may not happen exactly as you envisioned them or on the time line that you picked out. Your plans might not unfold in an order that makes sense to you, but none of that will change the end result. When God says that something is going to happen, it will happen.

> Your hope, dreams, and plans are in the very best hands.

You may feel frustrated when you have to take a sharp left turn or go on what feels like an agonizingly long detour, but don't lose faith. Keep reminding yourself that God is in control. His word is reality itself, and if He says that something is to be, it will be. Your dreams and plans are in the best hands.

God's timing is always better than your timing. His plans are always better than the plans you make. His dreams for you echo down throughout generations. You may not live to see the end result of your biggest dream, but God will be there, celebrating your job well done in His name.

How do you think your dream will impact future generations? Is there something you hope God will do with it after you've been called home someday?

....

....

....

....

....

....

....

....

....

....

....

....

74

Dreams Fulfilled

*The LORD will fulfill his purpose
for me; your steadfast love, O
LORD, endures forever. Do not
forsake the work of your hands.*
PSALM 138:8 ESV

When you reach the end of your road and finally see that dream you've worked so hard for made whole, it is an incredible feeling. Seeing your purpose and plans fulfilled gives you the tiniest taste of how God must feel when He sees all of His plans come to fruition. It's worth celebrating. Pat yourself on the back, and throw a little party. Take time to rest and revel in what you've accomplished with God.

Celebrate how far you have come.

Soon enough, there will be another dream growing in your heart, another purpose longing to be fulfilled. Are you ready for it?

This isn't your first dream to be made a reality, and it won't be your last. List out all of the things about where you are right now that show your past dreams and desires fulfilled.

Come back to this list when you need a reminder of what you can accomplish when you dream with God.

....

....

....

....

....

....

....

....

....

....

....

....

....

....

....

....

15

Praise God

*I will praise the name of God with a song; I
will magnify him with thanksgiving.*

PSALM 69:30 ESV

God is so good. He's with you when you're dreaming, when you're
working, when you're mourning, when you're celebrating, and
when you're needing hope. He is ever faithful. He gives you dreams as gifts to inspire
you, challenge you, show you what you're
made of, and draw you ever closer to Him.
Take some time today to praise Him for all
that He has accomplished through you. Here
are some verses to get you started.

> God is
> incredibly and
> marvelously
> good.

- Exodus 15:2
- Deuteronomy 10:21
- Judges 5:3
- 2 Samuel 22:50
- 1 Chronicles 16:9
- Psalm 35:28
- Isaiah 42:10
- Jeremiah 20:13
- Ephesians 1:3
- Hebrews 13:15

God is the giver of your dreams and the One who fulfills them. He's blessed you with wonderous gifts and experiences, and He's been there for every heartbreak and setback you've been through. He will continue to guide you, love you, encourage you, and bless you. Use this prayer to tell Him thank you for the dreams He gave you in the past, the dreams He's giving you now, and the dreams He will give you in the future.

Heavenly Father,

Thank You for dreaming with me. I couldn't have done any of this without You. Walking hand in hand with You on the path You laid out for me has been revelatory. I want to keep doing that for the rest of my life. I can't stop celebrating all that we have accomplished together in my heart, all that we accomplished because You planted Your dream in my heart and guided me, encouraged me, and opened doors for me to make it a reality.

Please, when You know that I am ready, gift me another dream. Lead me further on the path to fulfilling my purpose here on this earth. Help me to dream bigger and bigger with You, trusting that there is nothing that can't be accomplished when I'm dreaming with You. The world needs more of You. Please use me, and work through me to give more of You to anyone I encounter who needs it. I know my impact will be limited, but I'm Yours to do what You will with.

In Jesus' name, amen.